THE RIGHT JOB FOR YOU

Sponsored by Blue Arrow Plc

ROSTERS LTD

THE RIGHT JOB FOR YOU

DR JOHN NICHOLSON
and
SUSAN CLEMIE

ROSTERS LTD

Published by ROSTERS LTD
60 Welbeck Street, London W1

©J. Nicholson and S. Clemie 1989
ISBN 0-948032-63-4

Designed and published by ROSTERS
Typeset by Gwynne Printers, Hurstpierpoint, Sussex
Printed and bound in Great Britain by Cox & Wyman Ltd, Reading

First edition 1989

Blue Arrow Plc

Blue Arrow Plc is the world's largest employment services group dealing in the placement of permanent and temporary staff and executive search in a wide range of sectors. Subsidiaries of the Group include:

Brook Street
Blue Arrow Personnel Services
Extrastaff
Hoggett Bowers
Manpower

About the authors

Dr John Nicholson is Managing Director of an international Human Resources consultancy. He taught Psychology at the universities of Oxford and London and has written eight books, four of which had TV series based on them. Susan Clemie studied Psychology at Edinburgh University and is currently an Account Manager at John Nicholson Associates Ltd. She is a former international sprinter.

Acknowledgements

We are grateful to our colleagues Lesley Cowan and Carmen Harris for their assistance and support in the researching and writing of this book. We are also grateful to the *Sunday Times* and *Issues* magazine for permission to use material drawn from articles by the first author which appeared in those publications.

Contents

INTRODUCTION

This is a book about **Job Hunting**. So if you're coming to the end of the formal education stage of your life and heading for what your parents insist on calling the **real world**, this is the book for you. Read it and you'll emerge better equipped to cope with the job market jungle. Forget all those horror stories about interviewers being malevolent sadists, and short lists with a hundred names on them. Read on and find out just how to go about getting the right job for you.

We can't guarantee that reading this book will make the transition from education to employment completely hassle-free. You **will** come across pitfalls and barriers, but we'll help you to think carefully about the next step and with this forward planning you should be able to take most of them in your stride.

Most people find that the thought of leaving school or college begins to lose its attraction as the day looms ever nearer. This is especially true for those of you who leave school without any clear idea of what you'd like to do. Suddenly the outside world doesn't seem full of exciting and challenging opportunities. Instead it has become a minefield of threatening situations, and important decisions.

YOUR OPTIONS

This is the point in life where you first come up against the overwhelming number of options that independence and self-sufficiency have to offer. It is often a doubly difficult time, because you also have to cope with the physical and emotional changes that go with becoming a fully paid-up member of the adult world.

Don't let yourself get bogged down in all this confusion. Read the rest of this book and you should develop a clearer picture of who you are, what your interests and ambitions are, and what skills and achievements you can exploit. With this new found self awareness you can go in search of the kind of job which suits **you**.

Maybe you are leaving school or college in the near future and want to make some early plans. Perhaps you're already in your first job but hating it, and unable to decide where to go next. If you're looking for a job, and not just any job but one that's right for you, this is the book for you.

Waking up to the sound of an alarm clock five mornings a week is not the only life-change you'll experience when you start your first job. Nor will the most important aspect of your working life be the weekly or monthly pay checks that arrive in your bank account. The opportunities a job offers for you to become more independent, develop new skills and interests, and make new friends are just as important. A lot of research evidence points to the importance of this period in people's lives for the development of friendship. Young adulthood is the time when you are most likely to make close friends, and there is a good chance that the friends you acquire now will last a lifetime!

PARTING THOUGHTS

Have a look at these two teenagers' accounts, one of leaving school, the other of leaving college:

Andrew, aged 17: "I always knew I wanted to leave school after my 'O' Levels. It was alright up to the age of about 13, then the teachers started to get all worked up about exams and that, and things got a bit heavy. By the time I was 16, I was pretty desperate to get out and earn some money, and start looking after myself . . . The last day at school was a bit of a let down really. I'd expected to feel really happy and sort of free, you know. It didn't feel like that though, I just felt a bit lost. I kept getting up at 7.45 for weeks afterwards, and diving for my school uniform. I hadn't bothered looking for a job, as my dad had got me a place on a scheme at his work. I regret that now. Carpentry isn't right for me really, but I don't know what else I'd be good at."

Caroline, aged 19: "I cried for two days after I left college. It wasn't what I'd expected at all. It wasn't as if I had been dreading it either. I'd been thinking about leaving since January, and looking around for jobs. I was a bit nervous about how I was going to cope with going out to work, but I was looking forward to not having to study any more. My first job was in a bank in the High Street. I hated it, just couldn't get used to the stuffiness of it all, and I missed the chats with my friends. I left after 6 months, and now I'm working as a trainee dental nurse. I feel a bit as if I'm just drifting around and not really getting anywhere."

Since leaving full time education, Andrew and Caroline have both come across problems in finding the right job. For a small percentage of youngsters who leave school to go on to further education at universities, polytechnics, or colleges, the path ahead is often much clearer. Choosing which course to study isn't usually too difficult a decision. Teachers and parents may offer advice, and universities and polytechnics are generally flexible about course changes if you have a change of mind.

CHALLENGE OF THE FUTURE

The choice of what job to go into seems much more difficult. Many school leavers are frightened and overwhelmed by the mountain of job applications and interviews they face. What can makes this worse is if you get the idea into your head that any decisions you make at this stage are final, and that if you make the wrong decisions now, you will never get a job that makes you happy. This simply isn't true. Certainly we'd all like to walk out of the school gates and straight into a dream job. But the statistics show how rarely this actually happens. By the time you reach the age of 40 you may have changed jobs five or six times. But if you plan your job moves carefully then you can use each new position to develop some of your skills and interests and move that much nearer to the job that's right for you.

So, it really is important to remember that although leaving school is a time for decisions, they are not irreversible. You can, and most probably will, make mistakes, false starts and moves in the wrong direction. But you can't ever be completely sure of any decision at the time you make it. So stop worrying about it and start looking forward to the challenge of becoming self sufficient and independent.

WAYS OF COPING

Not everybody faces the challenge of leaving school and finding a job in the same way. We are all different, with our own unique hopes and fears. However there are some common reactions. Here are five of them. See if any of them describe you!

1. The Ostrich

Some teenagers really cannot decide what job is for them, and feel overwhelmed by the vast expanse of different possibilities. When asked what they intend to do when they leave school, they mumble about having not quite decided yet, and scurry off to bury their heads in the sand!

Ostriches tend to avoid thinking about the whole subject of jobs, as it puts them in a tizzy. When they leave school they either hide at home and refuse to look for a job, or rush into the first one they can find, or the first one they are pushed into by parents or friends. They may strike it lucky, and find a job that suits them. But they are more likely to find themselves stuck in a job which makes them feel miserable, with no idea where to go or how to get there.

2. No-Hopers

These individuals are horrified by what they see as a lack of options open to them. Of course this can be a rational fear. Without proper qualifications or much experience, many school leavers do face a period of unemployment. People in this group tend to feel that looking for a job is a waste of time 'there are no jobs, and no one will ever want to employ me anyway'. And yet, even in the most depressed areas, some school leavers do manage to find a job. Our aim is to make sure you're among them.

3. The Tunnel-Vision Brigade

Rather than being overwhelmed by the wealth of opportunity outside the school walls, this group have their hearts and minds set firmly on one particular job, to the exclusion of all others. 'Nothing else will do'. They have a totally rigid idea of exactly where they're going in life, which often does not take into account their own personality, qualifications, and situation. Don't get us wrong. It's good to have ambitions and plans for the future. In fact that's exactly what we are trying to encourage in this book. However, it is not helpful to form rigid and unrealistic goals which you have no hope of reaching. Not everyone can become a Richard Branson or an Anita 'Bodyshop' Roddick! And it isn't a good idea to narrow down your choices before you need to.

4. Blind Followers

Other school leavers know exactly what job they are aiming for, but haven't chosen it themselves. Blind Followers are 'encouraged' by their family or friends to go into a certain type of job, often the same job as their mother, father or grandparents did. For these individuals, the family tradition weighs heavily in their minds, and they find it difficult to think about other options. 'If it was good enough for my dad and granddad, it must be good enough for me'. Alternatively, they find themselves being steered towards a job one of the parents wanted to do and regrets not having been able to. In this case, they're being used to fulfil someone else's dream.

It is **very** important to make your own career decisions. Taking the advice of family and friends who have been through it all before you can be helpful. But it's you who has to live with career decisions. So you should be the person who makes them.

5. Bright Sparks

Finally, there are a tiny number of young people who leave school with a realistic, clearly defined plan of action, which is matched perfectly to their needs, interests and qualifications. These individuals have taken full advantage of their school's career service, asked the advice of their parents and of people who are already working in the job area in which they are interested, and planned their job hunting well in advance. And if they're really on the ball, they will also have read this book just in case it alerts them to any angles they haven't got covered. Don't try to beat these people – join them!

WHAT THIS BOOK OFFERS

We'll begin in **Chapter 1** by looking at your personality. What sort of person are you? We want to help you find out a little more about what makes you tick.

In **Chapter 2** we move on to look at the kinds of things that interest you. How do you spend your spare time? What are your hobbies, your favourite subjects at school, your pastimes? The answers to these questions should point you in the direction of jobs which contain at least some of your interests. We all feel good when we're doing something that interests us, and there is no reason why our job shouldn't be interesting too. So we'll be looking at the kind of job related tasks you would enjoy doing. Whether you are a football fanatic, a tap dancer, a trombonist or a beekeeper, there is a job out there to suit you.

Chapter 3 helps you to identify your skills. Prospective employers will want to know what you can do. And of course it is important that you match your particular skills to a job which makes use of them. A good command of French is unlikely to get you far working in a butcher's shop, but it could be very useful if you were working in a travel agency. We'll also look at more formal qualifications as well, but if you don't have any GCSEs, don't despair. With careful examination of your non-scholastic qualifications, your personal skills, interests and ambitions, you'll be able to develop a realistic plan of action which you can use to sell yourself to prospective employers.

In **Chapter 4** you'll bring everything you have learnt about yourself together. With all the clues you'll have gathered from the previous chapters about your personality, interests, skills and qualifications, you will be able to build up a complete Personal Profile of yourself. We'll look at the kind of jobs that could suit you, taking into account all the aspects of yourself mentioned above.

Chapter 5 explores the practicalities of job hunting. From the moment you decide to go for a particular job, you should be working on your plan of attack. We will give you some handy hints about where to look, how to develop a curriculum vitae, and how to fill in application forms.

Chapter 6 examines 'The Final Hurdle' – the interview. Among other things, we'll look at how to prepare for it and what kind of questions you can expect to face.

Finally in **Chapter 7**, we're going to look at 'Making Your Job Work For You'.

Suppose though, you already reckon you know what job you're after and that a book like this can't tell you anything you don't already know. You could be right. Maybe you're one of that tiny percentage of the human race that has a true vocation. But it may still be worth taking a quick look at how you've reached your decision.

Was it a rational, logical process, based on careful thinking, which took into account all the factors mentioned in the previous paragraphs, including your individual personality, aptitudes and ambitions? Or were there a number of 'rogue' factors that may be making your choice less rational than you'd like? Were there pressures from parents, a teacher, or friends? And what about the state of the local job market? Perhaps you live in an area where you have more chance of getting a job in farming than in electronic engineering. It is very sensible for you to take your local situation into account when choosing a job. However, it is equally important to assess how well the job matches your particular needs.

You may even have based your choice on a set of misinformed, or even false assumptions about what a particular job entails. For example, some people are convinced they want to go into personnel work because they're 'good with people' without realising that an aptitude for administration is also a crucial requirement if you want to succeed in this kind of work.

THE RIGHT DIRECTION

This book won't choose a job for you. But wc do hope to help you focus your thoughts and feelings and to point you in the right direction. We'll help you examine your whole situation carefully and logically, so that you can build up an overall picture of yourself to match against the requirements and characteristics of different types of jobs. So if you're fed up being stuck for words when family and friends ask you if you've decided what to do with your life, read on! Decision time may be just around the corner. Choosing a job doesn't have to be that difficult. In fact, you may even surprise yourself by discovering that it can sometimes be quite an enjoyable experience.

CHAPTER 1:
WHAT MAKES YOU TICK?

What do people mean when they talk about 'personality'? You probably have quite a good idea of what it is, but find it quite difficult to put into words. Most of us think of personality as what people are like. This is based partly on guesswork (we can't **know** what it feels like inside someone else's head) but also on observation of what they actually do. And we all like to think that we're amateur psychologists, as we nod knowingly when a friend does something, and say 'that's just **typical** of you'. We act as if peoples' behaviour remains pretty much the same over time, no matter what situation they're in. After all, none of us like to think of ourselves as jellies that mould to whatever plate we're sitting on. In fact, as we'll see later, a lot of research evidence suggests that people can behave very differently in different situations a point which is very important in the context of a job interview.

Personality is one of the aspects of candidates that employers are most interested in. Many decide whether or not to take a candidate on the basis of their personality: 'You're just not energetic enough for this job', or 'We were looking for someone a bit more outgoing'. You may have the skills to be a secretary, the talent to be an artist, or the qualifications to be an accountant. But if your personality doesn't fit the bill - they won't even consider you.

We're all different, and it's just as well, because different jobs seem to attract different types of people. For example, you may not know many accountants or advertising executives. But you probably still have a strong hunch about the sort of people you'd expect to meet in the two professions.

FEELINGS COUNT

These hunches are based on stereotypes - sweeping generalisations that we use to simplify the world around us - and you should be careful not to let them influence your judgement too much. However, it is very important that you begin your search for the right job armed with a clear idea of what makes you tick. That way you can focus your search on the kind of jobs that are likely to make you happy, not just the ones you're qualified for or have an interest in.

It's very easy to be misled by your qualifications and skills into going into a job that just isn't right for you, as Janice, aged 20, found when she went to work in a High Street Building Society.

'From the age of about 9 I knew that I was good at Maths. Figures have never been any problem for me, and my teachers always advised me to use my head for numbers when I left school. The careers advisor I saw at the end of the Sixth Form took one look at my 'A' Level results and pushed me towards a job in banking. That was two years ago now. I work in a building society in my home town. Although I'm coping with the job, in fact I've been promoted twice, I just dread going in in the morning.

It's nothing to do with the other people who work there, they're alright. I just hate the work it's so repetitive and boring that by the time 5 o'clock comes I feel like screaming. On Saturdays I help out at a local youth club, and I'm pretty good with kids, so I would really like to get into youth work. It's quite a thought though, going back to scratch again. I just wish I'd thought about my career a bit more when I first left school'.

Janice fell into a common trap. In her search for a career, she took only one aspect of herself, her head for figures, as a clue to what job she should be heading into. Your skills, interests, and ambitions are all very important. And we'll be looking at each of these in turn in the following chapters. However, the 'real you' - your personality - is the combined total of all your skills, interests and qualifications with a dash of life experience thrown in!

Finding the right job is not just a matter of matching your personality to the **job**. You also have to be careful when you're choosing the **company** you want to work for. Most companies have what is known as a 'corporate culture'. That means they have a certain way of doing things, and they tend to employ a certain type of person. This is true of even the smallest companies. Some companies value independent, fast moving thinkers, while others value caution. Few employers will take on a candidate whose way of thinking and behaving is clearly at odds with the organisation's, unless they have made a conscious decision to broaden their approach.

PERSONALITY PROFILE

Are you a leader or a follower, an extravert or introvert, confident or quiet and retiring? The list of adjectives you could use to describe yourself is endless. Are you painfully shy and willing to do anything to avoid talking to strangers? If you are, you'd get a lot of grief in a job like advertising, marketing or public relations, because they all require you to sell yourself to strangers. Obvious enough you might think, but it's easy to be tempted by the glamour aspect of some jobs. Don't get stuck on the unhappy trail of trying to convince yourself and employers that you are a vigorous, ambitious and supremely confident human being if you're not.

We all exaggerate our talents a bit when we go for interviews. The important thing is to try not to pretend to be something or someone you know you're not. Instead you should focus on those positive aspects of your personality which would be helpful in the job you're going for.

But how do you know what your own personality is i.e. what kind of person you really are? How do you compare with other people? And how much notice should you take when other people make observations about how they see you? The last point is important, because you do need to know how you look to others if you are going to succeed in job interviews.

One way to get a more objective view of yourself is to complete a personality questionnaire. There are many of these, mostly based on sound psychological research, and their aim is to give you a rough idea of how you compare with other people on some of the aspects of personality most closely connected with success in different jobs. Here is one such quiz. What you have to do is put a tick against every statement that seems to describe you. For statements that don't apply to you, leave the box blank. Don't spend too long pondering any questions, and don't expect them to describe you perfectly. Avoid the temptation to answer according to what you think you ought to be like rather than what you actually are like! There are no right or wrong answers, and anyway, you'll be the only person who knows what you have written. So if you are untruthful, you are the only person you'll be deceiving and perhaps damaging, if it encourages you to follow a false trail on your job hunt.

1. I'd love to do a parachute jump. ☐

2. I don't like telling other people what to do. ☐

3. I prefer spending time on my own, to being in a crowd. ☐

4. I find it easy to set myself plans and objectives. ☐

5. I have lots of casual friends. ☑

6. I like to think about the implications of my actions before I make a move. ☑

7. I don't get flustered if plans get changed at the last minute. ☑

8. I think that my friends find me a bit bossy sometimes. ☐

9. I always write appointments down in my diary as soon as I make them. ☐

10. I find it difficult to make decisions. ☑

11. I like to finish one thing before I move on to another. ☑

12. I'm quite willing to listen to other people's suggestions. ☑

13. I find it difficult to get to know new people. ☐

14. I find it easy to put people at ease. ☐

15. I like to know in advance what the day holds for me. ☐

16. I'd love to travel abroad. ☑

17. I like to divide tasks into stages and then tackle each stage in turn. ☑

18. I'm good at getting things organised. ☑

19. I like to have the advice and support of people more experienced than myself. ☑

20. I don't like volunteering opinions, in case they are unpopular. ☑

21. As long as I'm with friends, I don't mind how I spend my free time. ☑

22. I like to try new approaches to old problems. ☑

23. I'm better with things than I am with people. ☐

24. I find it easy to make up stories. ☐

25. I don't like changes, they make me nervous. ☐

26. I enjoy wild parties. ☑

27. I like to wear the latest fashions. ☐

28. I don't find it difficult to work with different kinds of people. ☑

29. I find it easy to whip up a quick meal with just a few basic ingredients. ☑

30. I would prefer being team captain to just being one of the team. ☐

31. I hate feeling rushed. ☐

32. I am good at mending things that have broken. ☑

33. I like meeting lots of different people. ☑

34. I'm always full of good ideas. ☐

35. I blush easily. ☑

36. I have a lot of common sense. ☑

37. I would never volunteer for a task until I knew exactly what it involved. ☑

38. I don't mind where I go with my friends, ☐
    as long as they're happy.

39. I like expressing my feelings through painting ☐
    or playing a musical instrument.

40. I like to be fully responsible for anything ☑
    that I do.

Your answers to these 40 questions will give you a
rough idea of how you score on the different aspects of
personality. They also make it possible to form a few
preliminary impressions about your suitability (or
otherwise) for certain types of work. Let's label the
personality characteristics A to J. Each one is 'tapped'
by four questions, as follows:

Personality Characteristics	Questions
A *2*	6, 15, 25, 37
B *2*	2, 10, 19, 38
C *2*	9, 11, 17, 31
D *1*	4, 8, 30, 40
E *2*	1, 16, 22, 27
F *4*	7, 12, 21, 28
G *3*	5, 14, 26, 33
H *3*	18, 23, 32, 36
I *½2*	3, 13, 20, 35
J *1*	24, 29, 34, 39

Count how many questions you have ticked for each
characteristic. A score of 3 or 4 indicates that the
characteristic in question plays an important part in
your personality makeup. You'll probably find that
you have 3 or 4 dominant personality traits. These are
the ones you must be careful to take into account when
you are job hunting.

Now let's see what each of these characteristics involve.

Characteristic A: If you ticked three or more As, you could be described as a cautious individual. You are definitely not prone to leaping before you've had a good look! You would be well suited to jobs which take place in a steady environment, like an office. Your careful ways would be both useful and greatly appreciated in clerical and administrative jobs.

Characteristic B: Three or more Bs suggests that you are a follower. You don't like having responsibility for other people, and you would rather implement other peoples' plans than develop your own. You're an excellent person to have in a team, as you work well with others. You might flourish in the armed forces.

Characteristic C: Three or more Cs? Then you're probably a rather methodical person. You like order, and approach everything in a logical and well thought-out way. You would thrive in jobs which make the most of your steady thoughtful manner, e.g. work involving computers, accounts, or perhaps administration.

Characteristic D: If you ticked three or more Ds, you're likely to be a leader. You are confident in your abilities and you like to be in charge. You'd be well suited to managerial posts, and jobs which involve selling.

Characteristic E: Three or more Es makes you the adventurous type. You like the thrill of new challenges, and enjoy taking risks. City dealing rooms might be the place for you, or some other area where they value entrepreneurial flair.

Characteristic F: If you ticked three or more Fs then you're a flexible soul. Last minute changes don't ruffle you at all, and you find it easy to work in many different surroundings, with all kinds of people. Most jobs require a good dose of flexibility. It would, for example, be an asset for a member of the police force, a travel courier or a nursery nurse.

Characteristic G: Three or more Gs means you're the outgoing, friendly type. You're generally the life and soul of the party, and thrive on crowds and new people. You would probably enjoy working in public relations, in sales or in the recruitment business.

Characteristic H: If you ticked three or more Hs you're probably a practical person. You're good at organising, and also have a flair for making and mending things. Any kind of engineering job would probably suit you. You might also be good at office management or accounting.

Characteristic I: Three or more Is means you're the shy type. You find it difficult to mix with new people as you're not confident of your own abilities. You'd probably be best suited to a job in which you didn't come face to face with lots of new people every day, e.g. as a researcher or librarian.

Characteristic J: A tick next to three or more Js, and you're probably the creative type. You have a good imagination, and are good at music and/or art. The ideal jobs for you are those which allow you to make the most of your creative talents, like art and design, and advertising. Or you might make an excellent chef or photographic lab assistant.

It's unlikely that you'll have found your ideal niche in life from such a small sample of questions, but you may be able to see the benefits of doing a bit of amateur self-analysis. The important thing to remember about this quiz is that it is only the first step on the road to self-discovery.

The number of personality characteristics and jobs to match them is vast. So don't despair if you feel you haven't quite cracked the mysteries of your personality yet. There are so many variations in human personality that someone once compared the task of trying to measure it with the plight of a blind man who is asked to describe the elephant he is standing beside. His reply depends on which bit of the elephant is within reach of the spot where he is standing. If he touches its leg, he will say one thing, if its trunk, something quite different. It's the same with personality. You can 'touch' so many different aspects of it that it's hardly surprising many of us find it difficult to feel confident that we know what sort of people we are.

BEHAVIOUR PATTERNS

The solution to this may simply be to devote a bit more time to thinking about the question, Who am I? Doing so can help you understand yourself better. It may also help you see that other people are different from you, and give you an insight into how you look to them.

Try setting aside 20 minutes every day to think about the events of the day. Can you see any patterns in the way you behaved? For example, do you always react by flying off the handle when faced with criticism? If so, next time, stop and listen to what is being said, learn from the experience and put your new knowledge to good use when you're faced with a similar situation again.

Of course, we're not always the best people to keep tabs on our own behaviour. If you really want to find out about yourself, ask your family and friends to write down the five positive and the five negative personality characteristics they think describe you best. You might be surprised by how other people perceive you. Think about each characteristic carefully and make lists of the ones that seem to crop up again and again.

Keep the positive list handy and use it to boost your confidence in times of doubt. It will also be useful when interviewers ask you to tell them about yourself. The negative list might be helpful later on in this chapter, when we look at how you can set about changing yourself for the better.

If after these exercises in self discovery, you're still not quite sure what you're all about, don't despair. Getting to understand yourself is a lifelong task, and you will already have enough insight into yourself to make your hunt for the right job a lot easier.

CAN YOU CHANGE?

What can you do if you don't like the way you are? Most of us are unhappy with at least one aspect of our personality and would like to change. But can a leopard change its spots? The best place to start searching for the answer to this question is to look at what makes you the way you are in the first place. Psychologists have carried out thousands of studies, in an attempt to find the answer to this question. The evidence suggests that some of our personality characteristics (such as our general mood and energy level) are inherited from our parents. However, it seems that most of our personality is made up of a mixture of the culture we have been brought up in and experiences that are unique to ourselves. Mixed up with inborn predispositions and with the situations we find ourselves in, these factors together shape our personality.

All this seems to suggest that with a little effort, you should find it easy to change the way you behave. However, in the past, some scientists have been very cautious about this. Psychoanalysts for example, argue that we're all ruled by biological instincts, like aggression, and so don't have that much choice over how we behave. They also insist that personality is firmly set for life as a result of what happens to us in early childhood.

The idea that we are born shy, anxious, bad tempered, or whatever, is quite appealing, because it provides the perfect excuse for irrational or bad behaviour. We can just say that Tom shouts because he is bad tempered, or that Lesley becomes tongue-tied in front of an audience because she is shy. This sort of 'explanation' doesn't really explain anything at all. And it ignores two very important features of the way people actually behave. We don't react in the same way in every situation, nor do we pass through life without experiencing quite enormous changes in our character, even if we make no conscious effort to change.

In fact the bulk of the evidence seems to suggest that we can change the way we behave. The fact that you're reading this book says something very important about you - that you're willing to take a closer look at yourself. And that's only one step away from actually changing.

The most important question to ask yourself before you try to change is 'how much do I want to change?'. The amount of motivation to change or improve yourself varies enormously between different people, and even in the same person between one period of life and another. Some people seem to be perpetually discontented with themselves and their lot, while others are prepared to look on the bright side and make the most of their own personality and whatever life throws their way.

If you're about to launch yourself into a new lifestage from education to work it's pretty safe to assume that you are interested in making the most of yourself. So, let's take a look at a few tips and principles for self improvement.

PRACTICAL TIPS

The first thing you must do is decide what it is you want to change about yourself. Use the space on the next page to write down the five things you'd most like to change. Don't be too hard on yourself, but do try to be objective and honest.

Things I'd Like To Change About Myself

1. ....

   ....

2. ....

   ....

3. ....

   ....

4. ....

   ....

5. ....

   ....

Two of the most common candidates for 'the bit of me I'd most like to change', are shyness and the tendency to let people walk all over you. Find out if either of these characteristics is standing between you and the job of your dreams by completing the quizzes below.

First of all, shyness. Look at each of these statements and tick the ones that sound as though they describe you.

                                              TRUE   FALSE

1. I rarely worry about making a good   ☐   ☐
   impression.

2. Generally, I am very aware of myself. ☐ ☐

3. I am concerned about my style of doing things. ☐ ☐

4. I am not often the subject of my fantasies. ☐ ☐

5. One of the last things I do before I leave the house is look in the mirror. ☐ ☐

6. I don't often stop to examine my motives. ☐ ☐

7. I don't much care what other people think of me. ☐ ☐

8. I sometimes feel that I'm off somewhere watching myself. ☐ ☐

9. The good thing about being shy is that it gives you chance to stand back, observe others and then act more intelligently. ☐ ☐

10. When I start talking to someone, I always seem to find something to say. ☐ ☐

Scoring: For questions 2, 3, 5, 8 and 9, score 2 points for each TRUE answer and zero for every FALSE. For questions 1, 4, 6, 7 and 10 score 2 points for each FALSE and zero for each TRUE.

The higher your score, the more shy you are. A score

of 12 or more suggests you are ill-at-ease in the presence of others, and selfconscious even when you are alone. A score of 6 or less indicates that you rarely find other people intimidating, though it may be that you don't find them very interesting either.

Shyness often comes hand in hand with an inability to say "no" to others. Find out how easily you are manipulated by other people by looking at these statements and ticking the ones that best describe you.

	YES	NO
1. Do you find it difficult to say no to any kind of demand made on you?	☐	☐
2. If someone went to the front of the queue would you do something about it?	☐	☐
3. Do you usually put yourself second in family matters?	☐	☐
4. Do you believe that it is necessary to fight for your rights, otherwise you risk losing them altogether?	☐	☐
5. Do you make a point of complaining if you are sold shoddy goods?	☐	☐
6. Do you have great difficulty in leaving situations when you have had enough?	☐	☐

7. Do you find it difficult to get rid of a salesman who is persistent and wasting your time? ☐ ☐

8. Do you hesitate about asking a stranger directions in the street? ☐ ☐

9. If you were working on a committee would you tend to take charge of things? ☐ ☐

10. If you have been given poor service in a restaurant or hotel, do you always make a fuss? ☐ ☐

Scoring: For questions 2, 4, 5, 9, and 10, score 2 points for each YES answer, and zero for every No. For questions 1, 3, 6, 7, and 8, score 2 points for each NO and zero for each YES. The higher your score, the more assertive you are. A score of 14 or more suggests that you have what is sometimes called a strong personality. You insist on other people respecting your rights, and may even be seen as 'pushy'. A score of 8 or less indicates that you are submissive, a follower rather than a leader, and easily taken advantage of.

Take a look at your list again. How can you go about changing the things you don't like about yourself? A good start would be to ask yourself these questions:

1. Do I really need to change this bit of me?

Some people set unrealistically high standards for themselves, which they can't possibly reach. Don't be too hard on yourself. Nobody is perfect, and we all have good points. Some of you may have other people's standards imposed upon you by family and friends. Alan explains how he feels pressurised by his outgoing family to try and be the life and soul of the party:

'I've always been the quiet one in my family the odd one out. My two older brothers and kid sister are always rushing all over the place, seeing mates, going to parties and that. I always feel a bit awkward in crowds. I'm much happier sitting at the pictures with a couple of close friends, or just quietly reading a book in my room. My parents are always worrying about me, and trying to get me to go out and socialise all the time. They make me feel like some kind of failure, even though I'm actually very happy with the way I am. They just don't understand'.

Don't get caught in the trap of trying to change yourself to please other people. If you're happy with the way you are and it's not holding you back from doing anything, stick to your guns. Your family and friends will eventually realise that you're happy and come to respect that. If you're not happy, and do want to change, the next question to ask yourself is:

2. Do I need help to change this part of me?

There are many groups in existence which claim to help you change yourself in one way or another. There is assertiveness training to gee you up, and meditation or relaxation exercises to calm you down; there are social skills courses to make you more agreeable, and EST if you want to become more dynamic. Then there are encounter groups to put you more in touch with yourself, and if you don't like what you find there, an enormous range of therapies to help you iron out the flaws that stand between you and perfection!

If these all sound a bit too drastic for what you had in mind, how about a little self-help? Browse around your local library - there are a multitude of books offering to help change yourself.

3. Should I ask my family and friends to help?

Often friends and family unconsciously reinforce the way we are. If they expect us to be shy in new company, they will make allowances and treat us as if we're shy in every situation. Most of us find it very hard to resist other people's expectations. So you should take your loved ones into your confidence. Tell them that you are trying to change an aspect of yourself that makes you unhappy, and ask them for their support. The next thing to think about is:

4. Would changes in my daily life make changing easier?

Often simple changes in your routine can have a major effect on how you feel, and on how you behave. For example, if you'd like to stop being so grumpy in the morning, why not try going to bed a bit earlier? Sounds simple doesn't it? Of course it isn't always that easy. And even when it **is** a simple matter of changing our routine, we can be very resistant to making that change. You may feel safe with the way things are and a fear of the unknown may make change seem rather less attractive. But if you're going to make any progress, you must grab the bull by the horns. Being only half committed to the idea of change won't get you anywhere. Once you've decided definitely to make the break, ask yourself:

5. What's the best way to tackle the task of change?

The most successful way to change is to start with modest, carefully defined and restricted goals. Often the bit of you you're trying to change, whether it be your tendency to be grumpy in the morning or the way you blush and stutter when talking to new people, is so worrying that even a small improvement goes hand in hand with a dramatic improvement in how you see yourself.

One of the most important things to remember about change is that it isn't easy. It can be very stressful, a point you should bear in mind when you're preparing yourself for it. And even changes for the better can make us feel unsettled and scared. So don't try and do everything at once. Split the task into small sections and tackle each bit in turn.

THE ART OF CONVERSATION

Let's take a concrete example. Suppose you would like to become more at ease with new people, the first thing to do would be to start making a greater contribution to conversation with people you know well. Steer the conversation around to topics you are knowledgeable about and into areas where people are bound to ask for your opinion. Don't just give monosyllabic answers, and try to finish your contributions with questions to other people. This way, you come to be seen as the sort of person who can control a conversation, other than just being dragged along by it. You will find yourself being treated with new respect and your opinion of yourself will rise too.

Armed with this new self respect, you shouldn't find it too difficult to move on to the next stage - meeting and talking freely to *new* people. You should start by understanding that you're not alone in finding this difficult. Others may look more at ease, but in reality the situation in which two people meet for the first time is one which almost nobody faces without some inner doubts. What varies is the extent to which inner doubts are allowed to become visible. It is possible to learn to combat the outward manifestations of anxiety. Each time you speak to a stranger, it becomes a little easier, and you develop an armoury of conversational topics and social devices which you know are effective because they have worked for you in the past. The job interview is the classic example of a situation in which we improve with experience (see Chapter 6). But the same goes for virtually every type of social encounter. Even those lucky people who never seemed to find social interaction too difficult get better with practice!

If you don't seem to be making sufficiently rapid progress, don't give up. Because failure tends to stick in the mind longer than success, many of us become unnecessarily pessimistic about our ability to change ourselves. We remember the broken New Year's resolutions and the abandoned diets rather than our achievement of what may once have looked like impossibly difficult tasks, learning to accept criticism for example, or becoming more flexible in our approach to life.

By now, you should have a fairly good idea of the kind of person you are. You've also had a few handy tips about how to change those aspects of yourself you're not quite happy with. Armed with these insights you will be better equipped to go out and find the job that's right for you.

IN CONTROL

One last thing. One aspect of personality that will make an enormous contribution to finding and making a success of the right job is the ability to control your own life and to resist the feeling of being at the mercy of events. Here's a final quiz, to see how well equipped you are in this respect.

Answer the following questions about yourself, by putting a tick in **either** the 'Yes' or the 'No' box for each one.

	YES	NO
1. Is there some habit, such as smoking, that you would like to break but cannot?	☐	☐
2. Do you take steps to control your figure by exercise and diet?	☐	☐
3. Do you believe your own personality was laid down firmly by childhood experiences, so that there is nothing you can do to change it?	☐	☐
4. Do you make your own decisions, regardless of what other people say?	☐	☐
5. Do you find it a waste of time planning ahead, because in the end something always turns up, causing you to change plans?	☐	☐

43

6. If something goes wrong, do you usually reckon it's your fault rather than just bad luck? ☐ ☐

7. Are most of the things you do designed to please other people? ☐ ☐

8. Do you often feel you are the victim of outside forces you cannot control? ☐ ☐

9. Do you usually manage to resist being persuaded by other people's arguments? ☐ ☐

10. Do you laugh at people who read horoscopes to find out what they ought to do? ☐ ☐

Scoring: For questions 2, 4, 6, 9 and 10, score 2 points for each YES answer and zero for every NO. For questions 1, 3, 5, 7 and 8, score 2 points for each NO and zero for each YES.

The higher your score, the more in control of your life you are. A score of 14 or more suggests you have a healthy degree of autonomy, while a score of 10 or less implies you should be taking steps to get a firmer grip on things.

Let's quickly review what we've covered in this chapter before moving on to look at the ways you spend your free time.

SUMMARY

WE COVERED:
- the importance of taking your personality into account when choosing a job. You may may be the ideal candidate in terms of qualifications, skills and experience, but employers won't consider you if your personality is clearly not suited to the job, or to the company.

- ways of working out what makes you tick: psychological quizzes, self analysis, and the perceptions of people who know you.

- what makes you the way you are? The culture you've been brought up in, and experiences that are unique to you, mixed up with inborn predispositions and with the situations you find yourself in.

- ways of changing the bits of your personality you're unhappy with. These included group work, enlisting the help of family and friends, reading books, self analysis, changes in your daily routine, etc.

YOU SHOULD HAVE:
- a better understanding of your own personality.

- some idea of how family and friends see you; both the positive and the negative aspects.

- a better idea of which bits of your personality you'd like to change.

- an agenda for changing yourself, and some ideas about how to accomplish it.

CHAPTER 2:
WHAT DO YOU ENJOY DOING?

Maybe you're reading this on the top deck of the number 21 bus, on the way to the job centre. Or perhaps you've just climbed into the bath and are slowly sipping a cup of coffee and listening to Steve Wright In The Afternoon. Wherever you are, chances are you're reading this because you've got some spare time, you're genuinely interested in what we have to say and you think there may be something in it for you!

The technological revolution of the last 25 years has brought the washing machine and the microwave to the kitchen, and the computer and word processor to the office. It has also transformed our notions about leisure time, not so much by giving us more time, as by increasing the number of ways in which we can spend it. The amount of spare time we have varies according to our particular circumstances. However, most young people have an average of 40 hours per week to spend doing the things they enjoy outside their jobs. This free time is very important, as it gives you a chance to unwind and shake off the stresses of the day. However, it can also be an important source of personal development, if you spend some of it on activities which improve your skill and knowledge base. Not only that, but analysis of how someone spends their leisure time can provide vital clues as to the sort of work most likely to suit them.

A lot of people spend the majority of their leisure time watching television. (The average British adult spends more than 30 hours a week goggling at the box and in the Unites States the figures are even higher). Many however, prefer to spend their spare time more actively. Recently there has been a huge growth in fitness centres, clubs, theatres and leisure complexes. But this has taken place mainly in the larger towns and cities. If you live in a small town or village, it can be quite difficult to find things to do. Many towns have very few, if any, facilities for young people but most have at least one or two special interest clubs, like a Stamp Collecting Club, or Camera Club. And if there isn't a club which suits your particular interest, you can always set one up. Advertise in local shops, ask around among your friends, you'll probably find a lot of frustrated bell-ringers just dying to talk to like minded people!

YOUR SORT OF SPORT

One increasingly popular way to spend leisure time is to get fit by taking up some sort of sport. It could be something you tried at school and want to have another go at, like hockey or football. Or it could be something totally new that inspires you, like rock climbing or rowing. As well as keeping you fit and making you feel good about yourself, playing sport is a very good way to meet people and make new friends.

What you may not know is that the **kind** of sport you enjoy, or just fancy having a go at, can say something about the kind of person you are. It can also give you some useful clues about what sort of jobs would suit you. See what your sport says about you by taking a look at the following list. All you have to do is put a tick next to all the sports you've tried or would like to try.

1.	aerobics	☑	2.	football	☐
3.	squash	☐	4.	hill walking	☑
5.	weight lifting	☐	6.	cycling	☑
7.	swimming	☑	8.	yoga	☐
9.	cricket	☐	10.	handball	☐
11.	wind surfing	☑	12.	gymnastics	☐
13.	tennis	☑	14.	meditation	☐
15.	rugby	☐	16.	orienteering	☐
17.	fencing	☐	18.	hockey	☑
19.	riding	☑	20.	skating	☑
21.	basket ball	☑	22.	table tennis	☐
23.	skiing	☑	24.	netball	☑
25.	relaxation exercises	☐	26.	badminton	☑
27.	athletics	☐	28.	volley ball	☐
29.	diving	☐	30.	jogging	☑
31.	canoeing	☐	32.	water polo	☐

Now count up the number of answers you have in each of the following sections:

Section A: Questions 2, 9, 15, 18, 21, 24, 28, 32. *3*

Section B: Questions 3, 7, 10, 13, 17, 22, 26, 29. *3*

Section C: Questions 4, 6, 11, 16, 19, 23, 27, 31. *5*

Section D: Questions 1, 5, 8, 12, 14, 20, 25, 30. *3*

Make a note of the section in which you scored highest, and have a look at the interpretations below to find out what the sports that appeal to you, say about you. These are just rough profiles of the kind of people who enjoy certain kinds of sport, so don't be surprised if you don't fit the description exactly.

Mostly As:

If most of the sports you ticked fell into Section A, then you are the kind of person who enjoys team sports. You're probably friendly and outgoing, and you enjoy being surrounded by lots of people. You also enjoy working in a team, and like instant praise and recognition from others for a job well done. High A scorers also tend to have a large number of casual friends rather than a few close ones. And when they are not running around on the rugby field or netball court, they enjoy going to discos and parties.

Jobs to think about: personnel, social / community worker, receptionist, builder, policeman, teacher, nurse.

Mostly Bs:

Mostly Bs means you fall into the competitive sports section. The squash and tennis players of this world are often very ambitious. You probably set yourself high targets, which you often reach, as you tend to be high achievers. You can be rather aggressive and single minded individuals, willing to do **almost** anything to get what you want. Some high B scorers spend a lot of time rushing around, trying hard to get things done, and not quite managing it.

Jobs to think about: salesperson, politician, sports coach, researcher.

Mostly Cs:

People in this category tend to like outdoor activities. You are adventurers, and enjoy the excitement of taking the occasional risk. However, you secretly enjoy spending time quietly, on your own. High C scorers are often practical individuals, with lots of common sense.

Jobs to think about: park ranger, conservationist, stablehand, gardener, land surveyor.

Mostly Ds:

People whose sporting interests lie mainly in this category tend to like solitary sports. You are likely to be quiet, shy individuals. You're often self motivated, i.e. you find it easy to do things on your own, without outside assistance or encouragement. High D scorers can be fiercely independent, seeing other people's attempts to help as interference.

Jobs to think about: running your own business, book-keeping, librarian, nightwatchman, writer, postman.

What was your '**Sport Profile**'? Remember, this is no more than a rough and ready guide to the psychology of different types of sports people. As with all stereotypes, there are many exceptions, and almost no-one will recognise all of the characteristics of their profile. The main aim of the quiz was to open your mind up to the idea that the sports you take part in can say something about you. And perhaps the long list of sporting activities will have given you a few new ideas on how to spend your free time!

Of course, there are ways of spending your time that don't involve getting hot and sweaty. A lot of people don't enjoy rushing around chasing after balls or climbing up steep cliffs with ropes around their waists. There are many less exhausting, but equally rewarding, ways of passing an afternoon.

For example, most of us do some sort of reading every day. Whether it be the daily newspaper, a glossy magazine, or a classic of English literature, reading gives us room to escape from the pressures of life and relax a bit. Good books and stories don't just offer the chance to float away to a desert island with a sexy rock star or to lead an air squadron against an evil enemy. They are also the foundation of all knowledge. Perhaps because of that, most job interviewers are impressed by candidates who can talk about books they've read, and have a wide range of pastimes and hobbies. From your point of view, a broad 'leisure portfolio' should increase your self confidence as well as providing you with more to talk about and hence a better chance of convincing the interviewer that you are a candidate worth considering.

THE PAY-OFF FACTOR

But why do some people choose to spend all their free time pumping iron in the local gym, while others prefer shooting down space invaders on the computer screen? Why doesn't the idea of collecting train registration numbers fill every one of us with excitement?

The answer is quite simple. It stems from a basic fact about human nature. We saw in Chapter 1 that we're all individuals, with our own personalities and unique life histories. The fact that we have such different interests is just another expression of this. The surroundings you have been brought up in will also influence the kinds of things you like to do in your spare time. There aren't too many surfing fanatics in chilly Britain, just as the Dutch are not renowned for being hillwalkers.

Finally, how old we are also plays an important part in determining what pastimes we take up. Most hobbies have their own particular image. Bowling immediately conjures up pictures of old ladies, bending slowly as they attempt to roll their bowl in a straight line along the grass. In the same way, American football and rugby are seen as the domain of young, musclebound "He" men. Another factor which influences the type of hobbies we enjoy is known as the Pay-off factor. We tend to choose interests that satisfy certain needs within us. Whether you like to be surrounded by people all the time, or whether you prefer to be creative in solitude, there is a hobby which satisfies your needs.

YOUR HOBBIES

What are the payoffs **your** hobbies give you? To find out, keep a diary for a month or so. Use the table below to make a list of all the different hobbies and pastimes you take part in. Once you have done so, you may find that the exercise has not only explained why you enjoy particular leisure interests, but also told you something about yourself which could help you target your job-hunting activities more accurately.

HOW I SPEND MY FREE TIME

1. ....
   ....

2. ....
   ....

3. ....
   ....

4. ....
   ....

5. ....
   ....

When you've made your list, try and put each hobby into one of the following categories:

1. Those with **SOCIABLE** pay-offs, i.e. those which involve some form of contact with other people, like discos, youth clubs and nonsolitary sports.

2. Those which offer you **INTELLECTUAL** pay-offs, i.e. which make you think and use your brain, like computing, reading and bridge.

3. Those with **PRACTICAL** pay-offs, i.e. which include **using** 'things', like mending cars, stamp collecting and D.I.Y.

4. Those with **CREATIVE** pay-offs, i.e. which include **making** things, like painting, carpentry, and playing a musical instrument.

What do these categories mean? Well, if most of your interests fall into the SOCIABLE category, it suggests that the major thing you get out of your hobbies is being with other people. People vary in the extent to which they like to be surrounded by crowds of friends. Even the most gregarious amongst us likes to be alone sometimes. However, some of us like to be around people most of the time. If your interests fall mainly into this category you should certainly look for a job in which you meet and work with lots of other people, such as reception work, community work or being a personal assistant.

If most of your interests fall into the INTELLECTUAL category, you probably enjoy pastimes that make you think and in which you need to process lots of information. If you're just leaving school or college, and especially if you've just finished a horrific set of exams, you might have decided never to open another book as long as you live. However, you'll be surprised how soon you'll be hungry for some brain stimulation, even if it's only a quick read through Barbara Cartland's latest romance. If you're the thinking type, look for a job that gives you room to use your brain: computer programming, research or marketing.

If you are the PRACTICAL type who enjoys using

their hands, mucking around inside car engines and sawing bits of wood, the best jobs for you are those which allow you to satisfy your passion to pick things up and fiddle with them! Jobs like carpentry, window dressing and gardening are probably going to be more your scene than being a shop assistant or a deskbound clerk.

Those of you who claim that you can't draw to save your life might be surprised to discover how creative you can be given the chance, especially if you're dealing with things you're enthusiastic about. If **most** of your interests are clearly of a CREATIVE nature then you need a job which allows you to exploit your talents, like interior decorating, graphic design, cake decoration, or jewellery making. An administrative office job would be less likely to suit you.

Most people will find that their interests fall predominantly into one of these four areas, with two or three falling into some of the other categories. However, if absolutely all your hobbies fall into one category, it might be worth considering widening your interests to include some pastimes from one or two of the others. After all, employers are more impressed by candidates with wide-ranging interests than with those who stick rather single mindedly to one kind of thing.

Categorising your hobbies and interests in this way has another value. If you can work out just what it is that you get out of your pastimes at the moment, you can make some assumptions about your job requirements. When you're scanning the Local Advertiser for suitable jobs, it is important to remember that you should be trying not only to match your qualifications, experience and personality to the job, but also to match the job to your personal needs. And this doesn't just mean that it should pay enough to keep you in Levi 501s! After all, you may spend 50% of your waking life at work, so it's vital to find a job that, quite simply, makes you happy.

Of course, most jobs offer at least a little of all four of these pay-offs. A good example would be nursing. Nurses work with people every day. In carrying out their work they put their theoretical knowledge into practice. They also use practical skills when bandaging arms or giving patients injections. And they may have to use their creative skills if an emergency develops and they are alone on the ward.

Our leisure interests should have a direct impact on our choice of career. We are far more likely to enjoy a job if we are doing something that interests us. That may sound obvious, but you'd be surprised how many people accept jobs they're not really interested in and then wonder why they're sick of them two months later.

YOUR JOB INTERESTS

When you're looking for a career, it's very important to take into account not only your **leisure** interests, but also your **job** interests. To discover what these are, fill in the Job Interest Questionnaire below. With any luck, you will find that your job interests are concentrated on one particular category. Don't despair, however, if you're equally interested in two or more. That just gives you a wider range of jobs to choose from. It may well be possible to find a career which incorporates more than one type of interest.

It's important to approach this task with an open mind. Don't assume that because you've never built a bridge, you couldn't and would never want to. On the other hand, if, after careful thought, you are certain that you have absolutely no interest in a particular activity, then you should make that clear in your answers.

Remember too that this test is concerned with exploring your **interests**, i.e. what you think you'd like to do rather than what you'd actually be good at. One last thing. Try to steer clear of the 'Not Sure' category, unless you find it quite impossible to make a decision. Now consider each of the following tasks / activities in turn, and put a score in the box attached to each of them.

Place a 2 in the box if it is a task you'd like to do.
Place a 1 in the box if it is a task you're not sure about.
Place a 0 in the box if it is a task which you definitely wouldn't do.

What would your response be if you were asked to:

1.	Investigate the cause and effect of pollution.	☐	S
2.	Build a bridge.	☐	Eng
3.	Keep an up-to-date appointments book.	☐	A
4.	Look after children in care.	☐	W
5.	Book people into hotels.	0	T
6.	Do the gardening in a large park.	☐	O
7.	Write articles for a magazine.	0	I
8.	Supervise a work team.	2	Mana

9. Work as a holiday representative/ courier. ☒ T

10. Help a dentist carry out their work. ☐ Med

11. Organise a money raising campaign for charity. ☐ W

12. Rewire a house. ☒ Eng

13. Serve customers in a bank. ☐ F

14. Check the quality of products. ☐ Manu

15. Do book-keeping for a company. ☐ F

16. Draw illustrations for book covers. ☐ C

17. Run a job hunting course for the unemployed. ☒ W

18. Attend to people during an air flight. ☒ T

19. Handle the legal side of house and property purchase. ☒ L

20. Identify customers who are likely to buy a new product. ☐ S/C

21. Construct the engine of a car. ☐ Eng

22. Use a computer to analyse statistical data. ☒ Com

23. Package goods ready for distribution. ☐ Manu

24. Teach people to ride horses. ☒ O

25. Make travel and accommodation arrangements. ☒ A

26. Show people around historic buildings/places of interest. ☑ T

27. Research into what preserves to use in food products. ☐ S

28. Plan and arrange shop window displays. ☐ C

29. Apply makeup to actors/actresses for TV, theatre shows. ☐ C

30. Assist doctors during an operation. ☐ Med

31. Check and research legal documents for a court case. ☐ L

32. Breed animals for show purposes. ☐ O

33. Help research and develop a new product. ☐ Manu

34. Install a computer system in an office. ☐ Com

35. Set and mark questions for tests/exams. ☐ Ed

36. Advise people about the use and side effects of medicine. ☐ Med

37. Present facts in an stimulating way to encourage interest in a subject. ☐ Ed

38. Question a suspect about a theft. ☐ Ser

39. Type letters and memos for a company. ☐ A

40. Advise people on how to save/invest their money wisely. ☐ F

41. Learn a computer language. ☐ Com

42. Present children's TV programmes. ☐ I

43. Produce and analyse financial statistics for a company. ☐ F

44. Collect data and store it in an information system (on a computer). ☐ Com

45. Interview and recruit job applicants. ☐ Mana

46. Collect and study fossils. ☐ S

47. Operate a machine on a production line. ☐ Manu

48. Design clothing/clothes patterns. ☐ C

49. Help children with learning problems. ☐ Ed

50. Control crowds at protests/demonstrations. ☐ Ser

51. Delegate responsibilities to employees. ☐ Mana

52. Store and catalogue government records. ☐ A

53. Represent your company at an exhibition. ☐ S/C

54. Analyse blood samples. ☐ S

55. Attend to the needs of elderly or physically handicapped people. ☐ W

56. Help organise exhibitions and conferences. ☐ I

57. Teach children to read. ☐ Ed

58. Look out for shoplifters in a big department store. ☐ Ser

59. Work on a farm.	☐ O
60. Train to use defensive weapons in the army.	☐ Ser
61. Look after children in care.	☐ W
62. Report news events for newspapers.	☐ I
63. Give legal advice to people.	☐ L
64. Drill for oil.	☐ Eng
65. Sell goods in a shop.	☐ S/C
66. Treat sick animals.	☐ Med
67. Chair a committee.	☐ Mana
68. Cross examine witnesses.	☐ L

Now add up your total score for each category by counting how many points you scored for each of the letters or groups of letters on the left hand side (S, Eng, A,W, S/C, O, etc.). When you've done that, put them in order of importance, so that the highest scoring category comes first, the second highest second, and so on.

Before interpreting this League Table, we should decode the abbreviations. Their meanings are as follows:

S = Science
Eng = Engineering
A = Administration/clerical
W = Welfare
S/C = Sales/commerce
O = Outdoor
I = Information/media

Mana = Management
Med = Medical/health
F = Financial
L = Legal
C = Creative (art and design)
Com = Computers
Ed = Education
Ser = Services (armed forces/police/security)
T = Travel and tourism
Manu = Manufacturing

Now let's have a closer look at your scores. You will find you can discard some categories of work as areas in which you definitely have no interest. Having done so, you can focus your attentions on those at the top of your list i.e. categories in which you scored the highest points. Some of them may be unfamiliar to you. This doesn't matter. There are so many different careers, no-one could know about all of them. However, if you come across a job in one of your top interest categories that you don't know much about there's obviously a strong case for going away and finding out what it involves.

Here is a list of careers, which fall into each of the categories above. It's not an exhaustive list, but it will give you some idea of the variety of jobs available.

Administrative/clerical

Secretary/personal assistant
Archivist
Librarian
Receptionist
Government administrator (Civil Servant)

Welfare

Social worker
Residential care worker:
elderly
physically/mentally handicapped etc.
Charity worker
Minister
Youth worker
Careers officer

Sales/commerce

Marketing
Sales representative
Shop assistant
Telephone sales clerk
Conference and exhibition organiser
Estate agent
Insurance sales
Publicity officer
Market stallholder

Outdoor/physical

P.E teacher
Farmer/farm worker
Gardening/landscape gardening
Running kennels/stables etc.
Horticulturist
Professional sportsperson
Outward bound course instructor
Forester
Gamekeeper
Zoo keeper
Stablehand/groom

Trainer of guide dogs

Science

Biologist/ecologist
Physicist/astronomer
Chemist/pharmaceutical scientist
Laboratory assistant
Mathematician
Geologist

Engineering and construction

Civil engineer
Architect/technician
Mechanical engineer
Electrical engineer
Carpenter
Plumber
Painter and decorator
Electrician
Surveyor
Electrical fitter
Electronics assembler

Information/media

News reporter
Writer
Presenter
Advertising
Public Relations
Author
Editor
Media resources officer

Journalist

Management

Supervisor
Foreman
Trainee manager
Management consultant

Creative

Photographer
Graphic designer
Interior designer
Furniture
Window dresser
Hairdresser
Illustrator
Model
Makeup artist
Musician
Actor

Financial/related

Bank clerk
Insurance salesperson
Accountant
Bookkeeper
Auditor
Trader

Medical/related

Doctor

Nurse/nursing assistant/auxiliary
Dentist/dental assistant/technician/hygienist
Veterinary surgeon
Hospital porter
Ambulance staff
Physiological measurement technician
Optician
Occupational therapist
Speech therapist
Physiotherapist

Legal

Legal secretary
Barrister
Solicitor
Advisor for Citizens' Advice Bureau
Company lawyer

Computers

Computer programmer
Systems analyst
Statistician
Mathematician
Data processing operator
Computer operator
Computer engineer
Computer advisor

Education

Primary school teacher
Secondary school teacher
Educational psychologist

Education welfare officer

Services

Store detective
Security guard
Prison guard
Policeman
Army
Air force
Navy
Firefighter
Manufacturing
Research and Development
Quality control
Machinist
Packer

Travel and Tourism

Holiday representative/courier
Hotel receptionist
Air hostess
Tour guide

JOB SKILLS

Now you should be armed with a list of 2 or 3 job interest categories, and you should have some idea of the kinds of jobs in each of them. The next thing to do is to look at each job suggestion in turn and decide whether it mainly involves dealing with **people, things, or data**.

Jobs in the people category include careers like nursing, receptionist work and teaching (the jobs within the welfare and education categories are all predominantly people jobs). In other words they all require good People Skills. Jobs which mainly deal with things, like carpentry, photography and electrical engineering, all have a practical bias, and involve working with your hands (like the jobs in the creative and engineering and construction categories). Finally data based jobs include bookkeeping, journalism, and computer programming (and include the jobs in the Legal and Computers Categories) and all involve dealing with information.

You will probably find that most of your job interest categories tend to fall into one or other of these three job areas. This exercise should have helped you to narrow down the job areas in which you are interested. If, for example, you scored highest on travel and tourism, education, and welfare, then you're a **'people'** person. On the other hand, if you were more interested in the engineering/mechanical, science and manufacturing, then you prefer working with **'things'**, be they objects, chemicals or whatever. If the categories you were most interested in were say computers, financial, and administrative/clerical, then you are obviously most interested in working with **'data'**.

FREETIME

As a footnote to this chapter, we ought to point out that the way you spend your free time is likely to change dramatically between school or college and work. Any of the following factors may influence the way you want to spend your free time once you're in your first job.

1. You will simply have less time to spare. Like it or not, work is going to take up most of your time, especially if you have to travel quite long distances to and from your workplace.

2. If this book succeeds in its aim, you should find that your work satisfies at least some of your interests. For example, a keen hill walker would probably find that a career in landscape gardening gave them all the out door exercise they needed. As a result they would probably want to develop some completely new interest.

3. Research shows that the majority of friends are made at work. When you start a new job you will probably be invited to go out with some of your colleagues in the evening. It may just be for a quick drink or they may ask you along to their flower arranging class or indoor cricket club.

4. The extra money in your pocket may encourage you to try your hand at something previously beyond your means. Not necessarily something really costly like learning to fly, but perhaps skiing or an activity which involves buying expensive equipment.

5. Your work experience will open up new opportunities for you to learn. You may well find yourself becoming interested in evening classes which are related to your job.

We hope that you now have some idea of what your interests are, and what you get out of them. However, this chapter won't have given you many clues about what you are actually good at - amateur footballers don't get to play for Manchester United, nor does an interest in art make you a qualified art historian! We'll have a closer look at what you're actually good at in the next chapter.

SUMMARY

WE COVERED:

- ways of spending your free time.
- your Sporting Profile - with job suggestions.
- the pay-off factor - what you get out of your Leisure Interests (sociable, intellectual, practical and creative pay-offs).
- job interests.
- the effect leaving school or college has on your free time and Leisure Interests.

YOU SHOULD HAVE:

- produced a list of your Leisure Interests.
- discovered what Pay-offs your interests give you.
- worked out your sporting profile, and seen what it reveals about jobs that may suit you.
- identified your Job Interests and have some idea about what careers they point you towards.

CHAPTER 3:
WHAT ARE YOU GOOD AT?

The aim of this chapter is to make you more aware of your skills, and to show you that careful identification of them can lead you towards the right job. Very often people don't regard the things they are good at as skills. They see them as things they do as a matter of routine in their everyday lives. So when we suggest that you ask yourself 'Where do my main skills lay?' and 'What are my real strengths?', don't be afraid to include even the most mundane things.

Generally speaking what you're best at is also what you enjoy most. That's true for your favourite sports and hobbies as well as for your favourite school subjects. This is mainly due to the fact that skills i.e. what we are good at, or think we're good at, are very closely linked to self-esteem. This is because when we're good at something, we gain other people's approval, respect and even friendship. This is very rewarding, so we work hard to keep on impressing them, in order to gain a further 'fix' of social approval and to heighten our self-esteem. As a result, of all this effort, we get even better at the particular skill involved. All this means that we tend to concentrate on what we are good at, rather than on things that need a bit more practice. As a result we sometimes neglect important skills, just because we haven't yet mastered them.

YOUR SCHOOL RECORD

Let's begin by thinking about your school career. What subject were you best at? Was it Maths, English, History, Art, or French? Whatever it was, it's easy to divide school subjects into various categories verbal, nonverbal, creative and so on. If you were best at subjects like English, History, or French, then it's likely that your skills lie in the verbal area. On the other hand, if you were best at Maths, Physics, or Arithmetic, then your skills probably lie in the nonverbal area. If you felt you were best at Art, then you posess creative skills.

Occasionally, excellence in a particular area of school work points you straight to a specific career. Take the case of Mark, aged 18, who had no hesitation about getting himself an apprenticeship as a draughtsman. He originally looked at architecture but thought that he wasn't academic enough to go to University, and anyway didn't much relish the idea of studying for five years.

"I've always been best at technical drawing, and that sort of thing. It was one of my favourite classes at school, but I was also good at art. I found that one really helped the other. Although you have to be really detailed and precise in your technical drawing, it was helpful to be able to imagine what the thing would really look like in three dimensions before you started on a piece of work."

Mark appears to know exactly what kind of job he

wants, and seems to have thought it out quite clearly. However, there are people who say they know exactly what they want to do but can't tell you why. Read what Sarah has to say:

"I've always wanted to be a nurse. And I've never even thought about doing anything else, I just feel that nursing is for me . . . I know what sort of things you do as a nurse because I always used to watch Angels when it was on. I think it looks like really good fun."

Now, if Sarah had chosen nursing because she felt she was a patient and understanding person, and if her best subject at school was biology, we'd have to say that she'd chosen her career wisely. However, she appears to be just drifting into nursing, without taking a realistic look at herself and her abilities. She could be making a big mistake.

CAREERS CONNECTION

After making a list of your best subjects at school, the next step is to find what careers use them. For example, if Maths was your best subject then you should investigate careers in banking, bookkeeping and accounts. If it was Biology, then you examine jobs like nursing, laboratory work, or physiotherapy.

To find out a bit more about which jobs involve **your** particular skills, look through the list of jobs given at the end of the SKILLS QUIZ later on in this chapter, and the ones at the end of the JOB INTEREST QUIZ in Chapter 2. They should give you a few useful pointers.

How can you find out what **non**-academic skills you have? It's important to remember that there are many other types of skills. So if you feel that you failed at school and never really felt motivated to work hard in any subject, don't assume that you're automatically destined for a dead-end job. You'll have other kinds of skills to offer employers though it **will** be more difficult to persuade an employer to take you on if you have no academic qualifications whatsoever.

Let's look at the broader definition of skills and focus on things you do well in everyday life. For example, can you cope with people even when they're complaining or becoming stroppy? Can you get along with different types of people? If the answer to these questions is yes, then you have good interpersonal skills. You may never have thought of your ability to talk to people as a skill, but it's actually an invaluable, and rare talent, much in demand in any service industry.

Think back to any school projects, voluntary work, or hobbies you've carried out in the past. What skills did you use for them? Did you do them well? What about the things you're involved with at the moment? Do they need any special aptitudes or attributes?

Make a note of all your skills in the table below, however trivial or ordinary you think they are. Here are a few examples of the kind of things you should mention typing, driving, computing, DIY, book keeping, writing. If you don't have any of these particular skills, wrack your brains. And if you're really stuck, ask a friend perhaps you're suffering from an attack of modesty!

MY SKILLS ARE:

1. ....

2. ....

3. ....

4. ....

5. ....

Every one of us is good at something, however much we may underestimate, or undervalue it. So if you still can't think of anything you're moderately good at, then go out and learn something new so that you can be! Remember how important a role your skills play in boosting your self-esteem.

Try not to set unrealistic targets for yourself. Often when we're good at something, we tend to be very critical and judge ourselves against very high standards. For example, if you're good at a particular sport then you shouldn't compare yourself with the current world champion. However it is a good idea to compare yourself with other people in your athletics club or school team, to get an idea of how good you really are and whether you're getting better. The important thing is to set yourself targets which are attainable and to value your particular skill.

SKILLS QUIZ

Have a go at this quiz to find out what skills different jobs call for. Your task is to rate yourself for each skill using the 0-3 scale below:

0: No good at all.
1: Not too hot, but given enough practice I could get by.
2: Reasonably competent.
3: Good, in fact wonderful, though I say so myself!

You may never have tried your hand at some of these tasks. When this is the case, you should use your imagination to guess how good you'd be, based on how you've coped with similar tasks in the past.

Tasks
1.	Interpreting graphs.	(A)	3
2.	Writing reports or essays.	(B)	1
3.	Looking after people in need of care.	(C)	2
4.	Persuading people to do things.	(D)	1
5.	Writing a poem.	(E)	0
6.	Wiring a plug.	(F)	3
7.	Dealing with money.	(A)	3
8.	Advising people on some aspect of their life.	(B)	2
9.	Teaching someone new skills.	(C)	3
10.	Organising people to do things.	(D)	2
11.	Designing new clothes, jewellery or furniture.	(E)	1
12.	Investigating a problem in a car's engine.	(F)	1
13.	Keying data into a computer.	(A)	2
14.	Translating passages from one language into another.	(B)	2
15.	Visiting and looking after old people.	(C)	1
16.	Motivating others to do a task.	(D)	2
17.	Painting a picture/portrait.	(E)	0
18.	Designing a new engine.	(F)	0

Now add up what you've scored for each of the categories (see the letters in brackets after each question). For example, your scores for questions 1, 7 and 13, give you your overall 'A' score, your score for questions 2, 8, and 14, gives you your 'B' score, and so on, for categories 'C' to 'F'. Once you've done that, write your scores for each category in the table below:

A 8	B 5	C 6
D 5	E 1	F 4

Now let's see what your scores mean. A high score in the A category means you're a nonverbal thinker who's more comfortable with numbers and counting than with writing and language. High Bs, and the opposite is true, you have good verbal skills and are a good communicator. If you scored highly on Cs, you're likely to be a caring individual, sensitive to the needs of those around you. Lots of Ds? You'd be good at motivating and managing teams of people, and would enjoy a career where you could use your powers of persuasion. And if you ticked lots of Es then you're the creative type, and one of those people who can turn two egg cartons and a sheet of sticky back plastic into a work of art! Finally, if you scored highly on Fs, then you're a practical soul, who's good with their hands.

SKILLS AND JOB MATCH

Later on in the book, we'll go into greater detail about the kinds of jobs which use the skills from each of these different categories. However, here is a very rough guide a preliminary 'match' between your skills and jobs.

MOSTLY As: NONVERBAL
Accountancy
Banking
Computer programming

MOSTLY Bs: VERBAL
Law
Journalism
Media

MOSTLY Cs: CARING
Social work
Nursery nursing
Community work

MOSTLY Ds: INFLUENCE
Sales
Marketing
Management

MOSTLY Es: CREATIVE
Designing
Acting
Writing

MOSTLY Fs: ELECTRICAL/MECHANICAL
Mechanical engineer
Electrical engineer
Electronics technician

We should stress here that all the jobs above involve using more than just one skill. Their category reflects the skill the job involves *most*. Take, for example accountancy, which is at the top of the nonverbal list. This type of work certainly involves dealing with figures, but it also involves a fair amount of contact with people, so verbal skills would also be an asset.

Also, the quiz doesn't cover certain skills, like those required for jobs in typing, welding or driving. These are the kind of skills we make a definite decision to learn, and which are usually gained through practice and experience. This quiz was concerned more with 'natural' skills.

If your results suggest that you are equally good at more than one thing, this is all to the good. Most jobs involve using several different skills at once. Even professional footballers, for example, need self-discipline and good interpersonal skills if they are going to make the most of their specialised athletic skills.

COMBINATION CONUNDRUM

The next step is to look at the way your skills **are combined** and to try to match them to particular jobs. Suppose, for example, you find that your two highest scoring skills on the quiz are Non-verbal (numerical) and Caring. How on earth can you get a job that will make the most of both these skills together? At first glance it may seem quite a tall order. But with a little bit of thought, several possibilities emerge. For example, one solution would be to train as an accountant in the National Health Service. Or how about book-keeping for a charity?

Let's take another example. What if your two highest scores were on E (Creative) and D (Influencing). What options do you have? The answer is plenty! How about designing clothes or jewellery and selling what you make in a market. You could even set up a more formal sales outlet somewhere. You would then be using your creative skills to produce the goods, and your power of influence in marketing and selling them.

With a little bit of thought then, it is possible to find a job which exploits your unique combination of skills. And it's obviously a good idea to do this, as you're more likely to do a job well if you can call on talents you've already developed. This doesn't mean that you can't develop new skills and improve existing ones within the context of your job. Part of the challenge of any job is that it calls upon you to widen your range of skills. However, if you go into a job without any background knowledge at all, the chances are that you'll find it hard to cope with the demands it makes upon you.

Are there any other kinds of skills you should take into account when searching for a career? What about **Life Skills**, which are arguably even more relevant to working life than academic and practical skills? These skills are closely related to your personality. They include things like how well you run your life, or how quickly you adapt to changes in your life. In other words are you flexible and adaptable, willing to try out new things? Or do you cower in the nearest corner when anyone so much as mentions the possibility of change?

LIFE SKILLS QUIZ

Try this quiz to see how well you swing with the changes. Which of the following statements sound as though they describe your attitude?

	YES	NO
1. I often wish people would be more definite about things.	☐	☐
2. It's not always necessary to make sure that your work is carefully planned.	☐	☐
3. I do sympathise with people who can't make up their minds about what they really believe.	☑	☐
4. I think a well ordered pattern of life, regular hours suits me best.	☐	☐
5. We'd be lost without words like 'probably' 'approximately' and 'perhaps'.	☐	☐
6. The trouble with many people is that they take things too seriously.	☐	☐
7. People who seem unsure or uncertain about the world make me feel uncomfortable.	☐	☐
8. I try to keep an open mind about things.	☐	☐
9. I always finish what I start.	☐	☐

10. I like to have a place for everything ☐ ☐
and everything in its place.

Scoring: For questions 2, 3, 5, 6, and 8, score 2 points for each YES answer and zero for every NO. For questions 1, 4, 7, 9 and 10, score 2 points for each NO and zero for every YES answer.

The higher your score, the more flexible you are. A score of 14 or more suggests that you are quite well-equipped to handle change, while a score of 6 or less implies a degree of rigidity and a reluctance to consider alterations, which may make it difficult for you to change yourself.

Don't be too concerned if you do find it difficult to adapt to changes or to make changes to bits of you which you're unhappy with. Have another look at the hints on changing your personality in Chapter 1. Once you've decided to make a change in your life, however, remember that changes *are* stressful, even changes for the better. So don't be too hard on yourself if you find yourself longing for things old and familiar. Change does take longer than you think, but even a little progress towards your goal can be very rewarding.

YOUR SOCIAL SKILLS

One very important life skill is the ability to get along with other people. This will obviously have a major impact on how well you get on at work. Jill, aged 17, a secretary, tells us how unhappy she was in her first job after leaving school:

"I was miserable. I'm very shy and find it hard to make friends. I really enjoyed the work itself, but I was just so unhappy because everyone was so unfriendly and no-one would talk to me. Then I heard another girl in the typing pool say she thought I was stuck up. I couldn't believe my ears."

So, although Jill enjoyed her day-to-day work, she didn't get along with the people around her. As it happens, they were misjudging her, thinking that she was arrogant when she was actually extremely shy. It was a sad experience for her, but one she learned from. The next job she went to she made much more of an effort to get along with people, and found that she fitted well into her new company.

Jill did it by making a conscious effort to improve her **Social Skills**. She followed a few simple rules. For example:

Be friendly. If you make an effort to smile and talk to people, then they're not going to be so nervous about talking to you, and won't be so likely to think that you're unfriendly or stuck up.

Try not to talk too much. It's good to show that you're not tongue-tied, but not to the point where people complain that it's impossible to get a word in edgeways!

Try to encourage others to talk about what they know and what they feel. The more people tell you about themselves, the more they like you. Good listeners are always popular, since they come across as interested in what the other person has to say. This is something most people take as a great compliment.

GETTING TECHNICAL

Another group of skills which are increasingly important are basic **Technical Skills**. You don't need a degree in electrical engineering to get a job, but it's vital to know the basic office technical skills, eg. how photocopiers, phone systems, and so on, operate. So be on your guard against that peculiarly late 20th Century disease, Technophobia! It can put the job-seeker at a definite disadvantage, for in today's world, a blindspot for technical matters is a real turn-off for potential employers. Typewriters have replaced pens and paper, but are now themselves being replaced by word processors. These machines get more sophisticated by the week, and it's useful to keep up with those changes.

Here are some questions designed to help you decide whether or not you suffer from Technophobia. Indicate with a tick whether or not you agree with the following statements.

AGREE/DISAGREE

1. When a telephone answering machine invites me to leave a message, I usually hang up. ☐ ☐

2. You have to laugh at people who think that microwave ovens are dangerous. ☐ ☐

3. Digital watches may suit some people, but I prefer to be able to see the whole watchface. ☐ ☐

4. I can't understand why some
   people seem to find it difficult
   to tape the right programme on
   a videocassette recorder. ☐ ☐

5. If I ring up to find out train times, ☐ ☐
   it annoys me to get a recorded
   message instead of talking to
   a real person.

6. I like supermarkets with automatic ☐ ☐
   checkout systems, because machines
   are less likely to make mistakes.

7. I don't see why people get so ☐ ☐
   excited about New Technology;
   the old ways of doing things
   are usually the best.

8. When I read about a new ☐ ☐
   electronic device, I usually find
   myself wishing I could try it out.

For even-numbered questions, score +1 for every
AGREE response you have ticked and 1 for each
DISAGREE box you marked. For odd-numbered
questions, score +1 for each DISAGREE response
and 1 for every AGREE box you ticked. Add up all
your scores.

The higher your score the better. The reason for this
is that even convinced technophobes agree that New
Technology is here to stay. They accept that the speed
of technological development is more likely to
accelerate than slow down. In these circumstances, the
ostrich position is not merely uncomfortable but

actually damaging to your chances of getting on in the world.

Fortunately Technophobia isn't an irreversible condition. The best way to cure it is to:

1. Make a list of the positive effects of New Technology. For example, it must be better to be able to produce a freshly cooked hot meal in minutes rather than hours, and to know exactly when the next train is going to arrive.

2. Look at some of the beliefs, all of them false, upon which Technophobia is based.

   (a) A fear that machines will take over. In reality, it is very unlikely that they will ever be able to function effectively without human supervision. Moreover, in countries with healthy economies, Hi-tech has increased rather than reduced the number of people in work.

   (b) The fear that machines are somehow less reliable or trustworthy than human beings. This is simply untrue – computers have been proven time and time again to be more efficient and reliable at routine tasks than human beings.

   (c) The final fear is encapsulated in the words: 'But I could never learn to work one'. New Technology is complicated, but the complications all lie behind the screen or inside the microchips. It's precisely this concealed complication that makes the human involvement comparatively simple. Research suggests that virtually all of us have the ability to achieve sufficient mastery of New Technology not to be handicapped in every day life, at home or at work, regardless of age or sex.

YOUR SKILLS COUNT

In this chapter we hope to have convinced you that your skills add up to more than just intelligence and having lots of 'A' Grade exam passes. Practical skills are extremely important in many jobs. Social skills are important in most jobs, but absolutely crucial in the sorts of jobs in which you'll be meeting and talking to new people all day long.

By now you should have a clearer idea of where **your** skills lay, and of what kind of jobs use them. Remember that any job is going to be made easier if you have a talent for it. So you'll feel a lot happier and more at ease in a job which exploits your skills than if you end up in a job which you find very difficult.

Having identified your skills, worked out what kind of person you really are, and knowing what your main interests in life are, you are about half way towards finding your ideal career. However, there's still plenty of work to be done! In the following chapter we shall be looking at your work values, ambitions, and achievements. But before moving on, let's review the ground covered in this chapter.

SUMMARY

WE COVERED:
- academic skills
- practical skills
- job skills
- life skills
- technical skills

YOU SHOULD HAVE:
- identified what your best school subjects were
- identified what everyday life skills you have
- discovered whether or not you are a Technophobic
- identified the kind of job your skills point you towards.

CHAPTER 4:
HOW TO CHOOSE A JOB

In this chapter, we're going to help you tie together all the information you've gathered during the course of this book. This 'personal profile' (your own unique mix of interests, personality and skills) should put you in a better position to pinpoint the kind of job most likely to suit you.

We're also going to look at personal successes. Whether big or small, we can all name some task that we have completed with a sense of pride and achievement. Next we'll be looking at motivation and ambition. What drives you to do the things you do? Is it money, a desire to prove yourself, a need for a bit of adventure in your life? And finally, we'll talk about what makes you want to work, what you want to get in return for working, and what sort of job you're likely to enjoy doing. But first of all we're going to deal with something we all have at least a sprinkling of – ambition.

What do you want most out of your life? Do you think your job will be the most important part of it, or will it simply be a necessary evil, a means of achieving your real goal of two weeks every year on a hot sunny beach?

Most people fall somewhere between these two extremes. They certainly want to earn enough to be able to buy a few luxuries, have nice holidays and enjoy a decent social life. However, most people are not prepared to accept a job which merely satisfies their need for money.

HOW AMBITIOUS ARE YOU?

Find out just how ambitious you are by completing the quiz below. Put a tick in the 'yes' box if the statement describes you, and in the 'no' box if it does not.

	YES	NO
1. Do you set your aspirations low in order to avoid disappointments?	☐	☐
2. Do you try to do things immediately rather than put them off until later?	☐	☐
3. Do days often go by without your having achieved a thing?	☐	☐
4. Do you find it difficult to enjoy a holiday because you would prefer to be at work?	☐	☐
5. Do you find it difficult to concentrate on an important job when people around you are chatting?	☐	☐

6. Are you inclined to be very envious of the success of other people? ☐ ☐

7. Do you try to enjoy work from day to day rather than struggling to improve your position? ☐ ☐

8. Do you often compare your ability and performance on a job with that of other people? ☐ ☐

9. Would you very much enjoy being 'in the public eye'? ☐ ☐

10. Do you allow escalators to carry you along without making the effort to walk yourself? ☐ ☐

Now add up your score. For questions 2, 4, 6, 8 and 9, score 2 points for each YES answer, and zero for every NO. For questions 1, 3, 5, 7 and 10, score 2 points for each NO and zero for each YES. The higher your score, the more ambitious you are. A score of 12 or more suggests you are hardworking, competitive and keen to improve your social standing. A score of 6 or less indicates that you place little value on competitive performance and may tend towards apathy.

GETTING MOTIVATED

It's not always easy to work out exactly what motivates you to work. However, it's extremely important that you understand what it is that you want out of a job i.e. what your work values are. Your next task, therefore, is to write down what you think these are. We've provided a list of possibilities to start you off. However, you'll probably come up with quite a few others. You may like to consider:

JOB SECURITY: "no-one has ever been made redundant here"

JOB SATISFACTION: "I love my work"

MONEY: "a fair day's pay for a fair day's work"

VARIETY: "no two days are the same"

PRESTIGE AND STATUS: "anybody would be proud to work here"

SOCIAL OPPORTUNITY: "the best thing about this job is the people"

ENVIRONMENT: "it's a fantastic place to work!"

TRAVEL OPPORTUNITY: "we have offices all over Europe, and we're all expected to visit them regularly"

GOOD PROSPECTS: "we're growing and I can see blue sky!"

FRINGE BENEFITS: "they really look after you"

Try to think of at least four work values – things you could get out of work – that would be really important to you, whatever job you had, and list them in order of importance.

MY WORK VALUES ARE:

1. ....
....
....

2. ....
....
....

3. ....
....
....

4. ....
....
....

This is a worthwhile exercise for several reasons. Firstly, you're unlikely to enjoy a job with built-in values that are radically different from your own – there is a close link between work values and job satisfaction. More importantly, work values are also important clues to your ideal career. Focusing on what you **want** to get out of a job, allows you to discount those jobs which clearly don't offer you what you **need**.

It sounds obvious, just as it sounds obvious that people

should go for jobs that suit their personality and that allow them to do the things they're good at. But you'd be surprised how often people forget their desire for certain job satisfactions and accept a job, just because it offers them a high salary, or because it's a 5 minute walk away from home!

And your work values will change over time. What's important to you now may not be so important to you in ten years time. For instance you might feel at the moment that the most crucial thing a job can offer you is the chance to help other people. But you might change your mind when you discover that you can't afford to go out with your friends on a Saturday night because your salary is so much lower than theirs. It's important to reassess exactly what it is you want to get out of a job at regular intervals.

WHY WORK?

Let's pause for a moment to answer more generally the question of why we work in the first place. The answer most people give to this question is 'to earn a living'. Work is a means of financing your out-of-work, leisure time. Yet that can't be the only answer. After all, people with loads of money often put in the hours, just like those on the bread-line.

Our society certainly puts a lot of value on work for work's sake. You'll have noticed that people have no hesitation about asking you what you're going to ' be' when you leave school or college. And it doesn't stop when you get your first job. Almost the first thing strangers will ask you is, 'What do you do?'. We make judgements about the sort of person someone is simply on the basis of the kind of work they do. The best example of this phenomenon is that of the much maligned 'tax collector', or the hated 'traffic warden' on the TV game show. You can almost hear the boos and hisses as these poor individuals admit what they do for a living. These kind of judgements influence our choice of jobs in ways that we are not always aware of. It's important therefore, not to be put off in this way and not to prematurely discount jobs you seem ideally suited to.

What other reasons are there for getting up and going to work each day? Other than earning us money, providing us with job satisfaction and so on, work quite simply stops us from getting bored. It also gives us a social life – the work place is an ideal place to meet new friends. Work can also help us to grow mentally, in the sense that most jobs involve us learning all sorts of new things. Not just complicated technical skills, but less exotic abilities like greeting people on the telephone. These kind of things don't always come naturally. And at work you can improve, for example, your conversational skills, even with angry or aggressive customers. And it's a useful knack to acquire because it can come in very handy in other areas of your life – dealing with irate parents, boyfriends, etc! So work is a great way to gain useful Life Skills.

You should also remember that getting a job is a matter of balance: giving your skills, time and personality to an employer, and getting back satisfaction, money, holidays etc. Getting is just as important as giving, so make sure you manage to strike the balance that you want.

YOUR ACHIEVEMENTS

When you're trying to work out what your plans for the future are, it's useful to have a look back at your life so far. Are there any outstanding achievements you're particularly proud of? 'Achievements' aren't just feats of incredible courage, like climbing Mount Everest or rowing round the world single handed with one arm in a sling! They're all the things that have challenged you personally. It doesn't matter if other people think they are trivial and ordinary, as long as you feel good about them.

Take a look back and try to recall those moments of self-satisfaction. Make a list of the four or five biggest achievements in your life so far. Don't worry if you can only come up with two or three, and don't be too hard on yourself. Once again, some people find this task easier than others simply because they don't judge themselves as harshly.

Just in case you're getting stuck, here are some examples of the sorts of things other people mention:

- climbing a mountain
- coping well with a particular crisis
- getting an impressive mark in an exam
- writing a good short story
- winning a tennis tournament

Right, go ahead, put your thinking cap on and come up with a list of at least five of your achievements to date.

My List of Achievements

1. ....

   ....

2. ....

   ....

3. ....

   ....

4. ....

   ....

5. ....

   ....

Now have another look at your list and see if you can detect any kind of pattern. The longer your list the easier it will be to see a pattern to it. For example, have you done most of these things totally on your own, without help; or were you part of a team? If so, were you the leader of the team, coordinating and organizing other people? Or were they physical challenges where you really felt that you'd pushed yourself to breaking point and triumphed? Did any of them involve you being creative in any way?

Whatever pattern your achievements conform to, they should give you some indication of the kinds of things you're likely to be successful at, as well as what you

enjoy doing. In turn, this understanding should give you an idea of the kinds of things you're going to be looking to achieve in your working life.

For instance, if several of your achievements involved organizing or motivating others, then you might well make a good management trainee within a large department store, since you've learnt that you possess leadership skills.

One of the most important things to remember when job hunting, is that there isn't just one job that's right for you. You may wonder then why you're completing all these quizzes and tests if, in the end, they're not going to lead you by the nose to your ideal job. Remember that although the aim of this book is to help you find the job that matches your personality, interests, skills, work values, etc., most people have the potential to work in several areas.

And there's a wealth of research which suggests that most of us are capable of far more than we actually achieve. Perhaps we can't all run as fast as Sebastian Coe, but each one of us could become a second faster at running the 100 metres – if we felt inclined to do so.

WOULD YOU RISK IT?

One of the things that stops us performing to our full potential is that we are frightened by the risk of failure. In today's rapidly changing business world, being prepared to take risks is no longer regarded as an undesirable characteristic. In fact, many companies now recognise that without risk-takers, they're unlikely to be as innovative as their competitors. So how do you shape up in the risk taking stakes? Here's another questionnaire to help you find out. Put a tick in the 'yes' box next to those statements that describe you, and in the 'no' box next to those which don't.

	YES	NO
1. Would you prefer a job involving change, travel and variety even though it was risky and insecure?	☐	☐
2. Do you tend to lock up your house carefully at night?	☐	☐
3. Do you think young children should be taught to cross roads by themselves?	☐	☐
4. Would you agree that an element of risk adds spice to life?	☐	☐
5. Do you think people spend too little time safeguarding their future with savings and insurance?	☐	☐
6. Would you always be careful to declare everything at customs when returning from a trip abroad?	☐	☐
7. When you are catching a train, do you often arrive at the last minute?	☐	☐
8. Would you make quite sure you had another job to go to before giving up your old one?	☐	☐

9. Do you often find that you have crossed a road leaving your more careful companions on the other side? ☐ ☐

10. Do you avoid 'thrill' rides such as the rollercoaster when at the fair? ☐ ☐

To score: for questions 1, 3, 4, 7 and 9, score 2 points for each YES answer, and zero for every NO. For questions 2, 5, 6, 8 and 10, score 2 points for each NO and zero for each YES. The higher your score, the more of a risk-taker you are. A score of 10 or more suggests that you enjoy living dangerously. A score of 6 or less suggests that your attachment to the safe and the familiar is so powerful that you may find change quite threatening.

If you did have a score of less than 6, beware! You could be narrowing your job options unnecessarily, simply because you are frightened you won't be able to cope. Don't rule out jobs just because your French is a bit rusty or you're not sure how well you can deal with difficult customers. If you want to learn, and if you're prepared to work hard, then you can do almost anything.

So if you find you're interested in something, but don't think you have enough ability, it is still worth a try. But if you have the ability and not the interest, then you should think a bit more carefully about it. Why head for a career in book-keeping if the idea leaves you cold? Don't get hemmed into a corner by considering jobs you're not interested in, thinking they're the only options you have open to you.

If you're extremely fortunate, you may be able to

make a living doing the kind of thing you would happily do for nothing, such as playing football, acting or writing. But you have to be exceptionally good at your hobby if you're going to be able to do this. Most people with a passion for playing the oboe, or a penchant for writing short stories, have to content themselves with using their full time job to finance their pastime.

YOUR PERSONAL PROFILE

Now that you've thought about your personality, looked for clues in your pastimes and job interests, thought about the kind of skills you possess, reviewed your achievements and checked your values and ambitions, you should be ready to develop your thinking about what sort of jobs you'd be best suited to. Why not check that you're working along the right lines by constructing your Personal Profile?

All you have to do is look back to the exercises you completed earlier on in the book, and gather all the information together. This profile should contain all the information you need to make an intelligent career choice.

MY PERSONAL PROFILE:
PERSONALITY

_____
_____
_____
_____
_____
_____
_____
_____
_____
_____
_____
_____
_____
_____
_____
_____
_____
_____
_____
_____
_____
_____
_____

MY PERSONAL PROFILE:
HOBBIES AND PASTIMES

_____

_____

_____

_____

_____

_____

_____

_____

_____

_____

_____

_____

_____

_____

_____

_____

_____

_____

_____

_____

_____

_____

MY PERSONAL PROFILE:
JOB INTERESTS

_____

_____

_____

_____

_____

_____

_____

_____

_____

_____

_____

_____

_____

_____

_____

_____

_____

_____

_____

_____

_____

_____

MY PERSONAL PROFILE:
SKILLS

_____

_____

_____

_____

_____

_____

_____

_____

_____

_____

_____

_____

_____

_____

_____

_____

_____

_____

_____

_____

_____

_____

_____

MY PERSONAL PROFILE:
AMBITIONS

_____

_____

_____

_____

_____

_____

_____

_____

_____

_____

_____

_____

_____

_____

_____

_____

_____

_____

_____

_____

_____

_____

MY PERSONAL PROFILE:
WORK VALUES

_____

_____

_____

_____

_____

_____

_____

_____

_____

_____

_____

_____

_____

_____

_____

_____

_____

_____

_____

_____

_____

_____

MY PERSONAL PROFILE:
ACHIEVEMENTS

_____

_____

_____

_____

_____

_____

_____

_____

_____

_____

_____

_____

_____

_____

_____

_____

_____

_____

_____

_____

_____

So let's assume you now have a good idea of the kind of job you want. If you thought that was the hard part, think again. You may have a set of potential employers nicely lined up in your sights, but you still have to convince them that you are the answer to their prayers. You still have to learn the best way to approach the companies you fancy working for. You'll probably also need to brush up your interview skills – what to say, what you're going to wear, etc. In short, you need to learn how to impress upon employers that you're the ideal candidate for their job. In the next two chapters, we'll be showing you how to do just that!

SUMMARY

WE COVERED:
- ambitions
- work values
- achievements
- under-achieving and the link with risk-taking
- your Personal Profile

YOU SHOULD HAVE:
- a clear idea of what your ambitions in life are
- a new insight into your work values
- a list of your acheivements to date
- a comprehensive Personal Profile

CHAPTER 5:
HOW TO FIND A JOB

If we have achieved what we set out to do, you should now have a better picture of the direction you want to take and of what careers suit you best. The next stage is to find out how to go about getting the job you're after.

The first step is to make the most of every available source of information. Talk to people who already do the job you're interested in. Go to Open Days and read all the relevant pamphlets and books. Employers are always impressed by applicants who have taken the trouble to find out extra details about their company. It shows that you've used your initiative and are enthusiastic about your prospects with them. (They won't know that you've done the same for every other company in the Yellow Pages!)

WHERE TO LOOK FOR INFORMATION

Let's look again at the kind of places you can find information about jobs. Asking people who already work in the field you're interested in really is the best way to find out what a job involves. And this is an especially good idea if they happen to be friends or relatives, as they'll be open and honest about the pitfalls of their work. Something to bear in mind is that each and every job has its drawbacks. The important thing for you to do is to weigh up the positive aspects of the job against the negative aspects. For example, if you like dealing with other people, jobs such as recruitment consultancy or personnel may appear attractive, but they also involve wading through lots of paperwork which could well drive you mad!

● **The company itself**

Another group of people who can give you real clues about what a job actually involves are company personnel managers. If your school sets up Open Days for you to visit factories, hospitals, etc., go along. Sometimes companies hold Open Days of their own, usually in hotels, where people interested in working for that company can come in and have a chat with company personnel about what it's like to work for them. These events are worth a bit of effort, as by going along, and appearing keen and enthusiastic, you can get yourself known. You'll also learn a lot about what particular companies have to offer.

● **Careers advisors**

If you're still at school, you should try to corner your Careers Advisor. They can give you advice on what booklets and pamphlets you should be reading. If you've already left school then take full advantage of your local Careers Office. It's quite likely that your Careers Advisor at school or the staff at your Careers Office will have contacts among the managers of local firms and businesses who inform them of vacancies. This is a good way of killing two birds with one stone school leavers find it easier to get fixed up in jobs, and local employers find it a convenient way of recruiting new staff.

If your school organises a Careers Fair, then you should try to get along to find out what employers have to offer. Also, if they arrange for people to come in and discuss details of their jobs, go along and listen. Some jobs aren't what they seem. For example, do you know what a calligrapher does for a living?

If you'd like to try some more job interest tests like the ones in Chapter 2, then ask at your local Careers Office about computerized tests such as Career Builder or CASCAID.

• The media

Very often you will see or hear of jobs through the media – through newspapers, TV or radio. Newspapers are by far the best source of information about jobs. The great thing about checking out job advertisements in both the national and local papers is that you start to get a general picture about the qualifications and the wages which go with particular kinds of jobs. The disadvantage of applying for jobs you see advertised in the newspapers is that you often come up against tremendous competition. Employers constantly remark how amazed they are by the huge response they get from placing even a local ad. So helpful hint number one for the job hunter who's really on the ball is to to get in there as soon as possible, before anyone else does.

If you know exactly what kind of job you're after and the area is fairly specialised, it may be worthwhile checking in the relevant trade journal. If you're unsure whether one exists for the kind of job you're looking for, ask your Careers Advisor.

And now that we've arrived in the age of screen technology, you can use your TV to help you find a job – if you're lucky enough to have a PRESTEL or a CEEFAX service. If you do have one of these services, make sure you make full use of it to check for local jobs. This doesn't mean that you should sit glued to the set all day, sneaking glances at daytime soap operas. But you should certainly check out the job scene at least once a day.

Most radio stations these days have 'job slots'. Local job vacancies are read out on the air, with information about where to go and who to see. This is usually of maximum benefit to people who are not working, since the job slots are often broadcast during the working day.

● **Job Clubs**

And if you've been unemployed for more than six months, a trip to the nearest Job Club would be very worthwhile. Not only do they provide you with telephones, daily newspapers, typewriters and paper, but the staff will help you with the wording of your CV, application letters etc., as well as providing good up to date information about the job market. And they can tell you all about the various government programmes that are currently running.

It's also a good idea to keep an eye on the notices in their window to see if they have anything suitable for you. They tend to specialise in sales and clerical jobs, plus a few unskilled jobs.

- **Recruitment agencies**

Recruitment agencies are worth looking in on too, since they often deal with jobs which don't get advertised anywhere else. The way they work is quite simple – agency staff collect details of your education, work experience, special skills and so on, and match this information to current vacancies in a way that best suits you and the employer. Employers are billed for this kind of service. But it shouldn't cost you anything.

PROMOTING YOURSELF

By this stage you should be armed with a list of all the potential employers you'd like to work for. So far so good. The next stage involves promoting yourself, or packaging yourself into a fit state to be 'bought' by the employer who offers you the best training, holidays, pay or whatever it is that you've identified as the work benefits you're after.

The first thing you should do is to make sure that you have a good CV (Curriculum Vitae). Then you should find out how to write a good covering letter to accompany it, i.e. one which points out just how perfectly suited you are to the particular job you're applying for.

A Curriculum Vitae is not as painful as it sounds. It's basically just a summary of your life. To show you what to include, we have printed below a CV for Sam Schooleaver which focuses on education and work experience rather than on such fascinating but irrelevant details as the date of his first step. It's absolutely essential to make sure you have a relevant and up-to-date CV on hand to send to prospective employers whenever you see a position advertised, or hear of one coming up.

In general, there is a standard format. Here's that example to help you with yours.

CURRICULUM VITAE

Personal Details:

Name:	Sam Schooleaver
Address:	13 Anywhere Gardens,
	London NW1 2AB
Telephone:	123 4567
Date of Birth:	10.3.71
Marital Status:	Single

Education and Qualifications:

Date	Name of School/College	Exams Passed/Qualifications	
1982-87	Secondary Modern School	'O' English Literature	B
	London, NWl 2AB	'O' English Language	A
		'O' Mathematics	C
		'O' History	A
		'O' Geography	B
		'O' Biology	B
		'O' Art	A
1987-89	North West College of	'A' English Literature	A
	Further Education,	'A' Sociology	B
	London, NWl 3CD	'A' History	B

Work Experience:

Date	Name/Address of Employer	Job Title	Duties Involved
Oct '87 - Jul '89	A & B Traders, High Street, London, NW4 5EF	Part-time Sales Asst. (Sat. job)	Serving customers, answering telephone, preparing sales invoices, stocking shelves, taking full responsibility for the shop when the owner left on various errands.

Skills/Other Information:

Languages – For the past year I have been studying French at evening classes and have reached the stage where I hope to take an 'O' level in the subject next Summer.

Driving Licence – I have a full driving licence and have been driving my father's car periodically for the past two years.

Leisure Activities:

Judo – I am a Brown Belt at judo and have been practising the art since the age of ll. Recently I have become involved with a local community group which teaches judo to young children under the age of l2. Apart from assisting the judo teacher, I am a committee member, and I help run the other social activities.

Reading – I enjoy reading and in particular have a fascination for science fiction. During my 4th year at school I won a second place Fiction Award after entering an inter-school competition with 6 other competing schools.

Referees

Mr A. Tutor,
c/o London College of Further Education,
London, NW1 3CD.

Mr B. Lawless,
Legal, Legal & Lawless,
73 Nowhere Lane,
London, NW1 4EF

Signature .... Date ....

Study this example, create a CV of your own and fill in your details under the individual headings. Even if all you've ever done between leaving school and now is to make out your first job application you'll be surprised just how much 'experience' you already have! As you can see, 'experience' takes many forms and any information concerning work, training or otherwise, which builds up a picture of your character and abilities is worth mentioning.

Here are a few notes to help you on your way.

• Personal details

The most obvious thing is your name and address. State your full name and don't forget to include the postal code in your address. That anxious wait for a reply could be a day longer if you don't. Another important point is to include your telephone number or a contact number if you don't have a phone or are out of the house during office hours. Large employers rarely use the phone for responding to applicants but small employers often find it convenient. Your date of birth is also important. Employers like to be able to see at a glance the maturity of the candidate they are considering.

• Education and qualifications

List the exams you've sat and your results in chronological order. Don't leave anything out, even if you reckon a GCSE pass in Needlework wouldn't be relevant to a job application for Telephone Sales. If you've passed an exam in any subject it says something positive about you and is worth a mention.

• Work experience

This covers all kinds of work experience paid or unpaid, full or part-time. If you've only ever worked during the school vacations, e.g. helping to sweep up in a shop, factory or office, put it down. No matter how menial or insignificant the task you took on, it all adds up to experience and demonstrates an independent and mature outlook on life.

Give the full name and address of your employer as they may be asked for references. State the title of the job and list every aspect of the duties that were expected of you. Once again, don't overlook any area of work you could possibly put down on paper.

• Skills/other information

Under this section you can come up with a whole host of things that might impress a prospective employer. A CV is a personal vital statistic which aims to attract. If all an employer has to go by is the information on paper before him, it is up to you to make sure that the information makes you sound as alluring as possible. You may think that your personal interests have very little to do with applying for jobs. In fact, they can sometimes make the difference between getting and not getting a job. An employer may have similar interests to you and might take you on or invite you to an interview because, apart from satisfying his other requirements, you 'seem' an interesting and therefore, worthwhile candidate.

Maybe the job doesn't require a driving licence. However, the mere fact that you have one says something about your character. A driving test is, after all, just that – a test and one which you have succesfully passed! Also, you may not have formal qualifications in some areas, for example, you may have shaky knowledge of a particular language. But if you are showing active interest by pursuing a subject outside of school it indicates drive and personal initiative.

What about school? Have you ever been a prefect, a head boy/girl? A position like this prompts favourable assessments of your character as a responsible and worthy individual. What are your interests? Do you read avidly or cook to perfection? Are you a secret poet? Do you have a passion for making model-aeroplanes? What places of interest have you visited? Have you ever been a member of any club or sat on a committee? Have you ever held any positions of responsibility or authority? If you are seriously interested in any area that involves personal commitment, mention it!

● **Leisure activities**

You don't have to be good at sports or hold medals to fill in this section. Anyone who doesn't consider themselves to be a living corpse can think of something worth mentioning. Apart from the obvious sports like football, cricket, rounders, netball, swimming etc., in which you might have reached a level of proficiency – you might also jog, skateboard or rollerskate. Doing any of these shows you take an interest in your physical well-being.

You may have noticed that employers often include a section on leisure activities in their job application forms. This says something about what they expect from employees. They probably reckon that an individual with healthy interests outside of work is more likely to show a healthy alertness while at work.

● Referees

Generally it's best to give the names and addresses of a teacher who knows you fairly well, and a well respected professional, such as a lawyer or accountant. Don't use members of your family. And remember to ask your referees for their permission before putting their names forward. You're asking a favour of someone, so it's only courteous to do so.

The way you *present* your CV is also very important. Make sure it's printed on good quality paper and typed out neatly with no mistakes. It's also a good idea to get your CV done on a word processor, if you can, because this makes it easier to keep it up to date. You should try to keep it as short as possible but without leaving out any vital information.

Having bribed/charmed (delete as appropriate) a capable typist, or sent your CV to a professional agency, you should then make sure that you have enough copies to send out to everyone you intend to approach, and some to keep spare. You never know when you'll come across the perfect job!

You would *use* a Curriculum Vitae when you are making a speculative approach to a company or when they don't ask you to complete either their own or a standard application form. Remember that your CV and your letter are all that a prospective employer will have to judge you on before they've met you. So take your time with the form. Write neatly – don't get coffee stains on it – and if spelling is not your strong point, get someone to check it.

COVERING LETTER

No less important than the CV is the letter which accompanies it. Every application form or CV that you send to a company must have a covering letter attached. But whereas a CV should take a standard form, every letter should be different to the individual company to which you are applying. The reason for this is that every job is different. The covering letter gives you an opportunity to point directly to your particular experiences and explain how these make you an ideal candidate for the specific job available.

In general, it's better to write this letter in long-hand rather than type it. This way the employer will realise that you have bothered to write one specifically for them, rather than sending the same typewritten copy with every application you make. As with your CV, it's best to use good quality paper **and** remember to re-read it to check for mistakes!

One more tip before we move on. If at all possible, try to address your letter to the Personnel Manager or to the person who deals directly with recruitment (many smaller companies do not have a Personnel

Department). Try to avoid addressing it to Sir/Madam and 'To Whom It May Concern' is even worse! A phone-call is all it takes to get the name of an individual to whom you can write personally.

Now let's have a look at a typical covering letter.

13 Wilson Gardens,
London NW2

22/7/88

Dear Mr Morris,

I noticed your advertisement for a Trainee Sales Assistant to work in your Aquatics Exotics Emporium, in the Evening Gazette, on 21st July.

I have just completed my GCSEs and am waiting for my results. I feel that I am a very good candidate for the job since on Saturdays I work in my parents' shop. They too are in the business of importing Piranha fish, so I already have a good basic knowledge of the various procedures involved in this line of work.

I enclose my CV to give you an idea of what sort of person I am and what I have achieved so far. I hope you will give my application serious consideration and I look forward to hearing from you very soon.

Yours sincerely,

Sam Schooleaver

When you find yourself phoning about a job you've seen advertised, always plan what you're going to say first. Write it down, so that you can refer to your notes if you get a bit tongue-tied.

● **On the record**

To stop yourself getting confused about who you've applied to, and for what jobs, be sure to keep a record of the advertisements you've answered. If you have to fill in an employer's application form, take a photocopy of it so you can remember what you've said. This could prove to be vital information when you arrive at the next hurdle – the job interview.

SUMMARY

WE COVERED:
● how to find out which jobs are available.
● how to approach potential employers.
● how to present the right image of yourself to a potential employer before meeting them.

YOU SHOULD HAVE:
● found out where to look for job advertisements.
● written or planned how to write your CV.
● practised writing a few covering letters.
● set up a 'log book' of companies that you intend to write to, and details of advertisements you've already applied to.

CHAPTER 6:
HOW TO GET A JOB

Let's not beat about the bush. Not many people enjoy the experience of being interviewed. But it's something you have to learn to endure and even excel at, if you're going to get on in life. Why? Because interviews are still by far the most common device used by employers to decide who they are going to take on.

Since we'll need to spend some time on this interview process let's divide it into two stages:

1) Preparation for the Interview

2) The Interview itself

PREPARATION FOR THE INTERVIEW

So you've done it. The Personnel Manager has phoned, or written, to invite you for an interview next week. Your qualifications and experience must be OK because you've made it through the initial screening process. The vast majority of applicants will not have been so lucky. This means of course that even if you don't get the job after the interview, you've done well by at least getting to this stage. It may not be much consolation when you don't get a job that you really want. But it's true.

• Research

Our aim is to make it unnecessary for you to look for consolation. We want you to get the job! But how? Well, the first thing to do on hearing you've got an interview is to find out all you can about the company. Send away for a company brochure if they have one. Read it from cover to cover so you've got a good idea of what they're all about. There are bound to be a couple of questions in the interview designed to see if you know anything about the company: for example, 'Who are our main competitors?'; or, 'What do you know about our products/services?'

It's interesting to discover what interviewers are looking for. Research shows that they are most impressed by candidates with a pleasing personality and a strong desire to get on in life. This is important information which ought to shape your whole approach to an interview.

So make sure that you can answer them convincingly and even ask a couple of insightful questions of your own that leave the interviewer in no doubt that you understand the company and its business.

• Questions and answers

The next stage involves a bit of work. However, after answering all the quizzes in this book and following the tips provided in this chapter you should be more than ready for your interview. You'll certainly be in a stronger position than most of the other people sitting quivering beside you outside the interview room. If possible, get a friend or parent to ask you questions as if they were interviewing you, and practice your replies. It's a lot easier than the alternative of testing yourself and replying out loud! Friends or relatives should be prepared to enter into the spirit of things, and try to catch you out by asking awkward questions or making you expand on the answers you give. This is excellent practice since you may get asked exactly the same questions by your interviewer on the day.

But what kind of questions do interviewers ask? Here is a list of some of their favourites. Not all of them will be relevant for the kind of job you're going for. Work out which are, and concentrate on them.

"Why do you want this job?"

"What skills/abilities do you think this job requires, and do you have them?"

"Where do you think this job will lead to in, say, five years time?"

"What do you want out of the job?"

"Which of the jobs you've done in the past did you enjoy most, and why?"

"Which ones did you dislike and why?"

"What do you think are your main strengths and weaknesses?"

"Have you ever undertaken a major project or challenge? What was it? How did you cope with it?

What did you learn about yourself during the experience?"

"Tell me about yourself . . . "

"Do you cope well under pressure? Give me an example."

"Do you prefer to work as part of a team or alone?"

"What do you want out of life?" (This is a woolly question, but it's the sort of thing interviewers ask at the end of a long day, so they'll be very appreciative if you answer it well.)

When preparing answers to these questions, you may wonder whether you're allowed ever to deviate from the strict, literal truth. The fact is that most people tend to exaggerate a little in interviews. They may even try to skate over one or two episodes in their lives that they're not particularly proud of. However it's unwise to lie about serious or easily checkable things such as your education or your qualifications. You'll be found out, probably sooner rather than later and no-one wants to employ someone who's a proven liar.

Exaggerating slightly just how good you are at certain things may be acceptable, however, and some interviewers expect it and allow for it. After all, self-confidence is usually a quality they welcome. But don't overdo it and when in doubt, stick to the truth!

One last thing. Make sure you have a couple of questions to ask the interviewer at the point, usually as the interview is coming to a close, when he/she asks: "Are there any questions you'd like to ask? Anything we haven't made clear?"

A fluent and convincing reply at this stage will show that you've given some thought to what the job involves and why you'd like it. Every job has different information which you need to find out about. But there are several general topics which you could intelligently enquire about, whatever the job. For example, training, location and salary. If everything about the job seems to have been covered already, then ask about the company or organisation. When was it founded? What are its long-term plans? Are there any major changes in progress?

● **Testing, testing**

It's also useful to prepare yourself for the tests that some companies now use for recruitment. Most still rely on interviews, but it's important not to be thrown into a panic if you're confronted by something a bit more scientific.

There are two types of tests you may be asked to do. The first kind are personality tests. Where these are concerned, the best plan is to answer them as honestly as you can, since most of them are really only being used as a device to spot serious personality disorders. As long as you're not pathologically disturbed, these tests should be nothing to worry about. Some personality tests are designed to test specific aspects of your personality, like the ones in Chapter 1 of this book. Most invite you to describe your behaviour or to guess what you might do if you found yourself in various situations. Answer them as truthfully as you can.

The other kind of test you may come across is the Aptitude Test, of which there are several types. The most common Aptitude Tests are:

Verbal: tests for good command of written and/or spoken English.

Numerical: tests for ability to deal with figures and statistical tables, i.e. basic arithmetic.

Spatial: tests for ability to judge shapes and dimensions.

Mechanical: tests for the understanding of basic mechanical principles.

These tests are particularly relevant when people are applying for a job they have no experience of. Depending on the nature of the job, you may be set a relevant test, so that the employer can see whether you'd be a suitable candidate for the training that the job involves. For example, if you were going for an apprentice mechanic post you might be given a mechanical test rather than a verbal one.

The best way to prepare for these tests is to practice, by using a book such as H.J. Eysenck's 'Know Your Own IQ'. You needn't bother doing all the examples from cover to cover. Just try 20 or so to see how you get on with them, since you may not have come across this sort of thing before. Check the shelves of your local library, especially the sections marked 'Jobs' or 'Education'.

Here are some hints on how to handle the test situation:

1) If you get stuck, move on to the next one. The tests are always timed. It's best to get as much done as you can in the time available.

2) Always answer the question. If you have to pick one of several answers, you've always got a chance of getting it right by fluke even if you have no idea what the correct answer is!

THE INTERVIEW ITSELF

● Dress the part

The first important point to be made is: dress smartly! First impressions at an interview are crucially important, however unfair this may seem. In fact, research shows that eight times out of ten, the decision as to whether or not the candidate (i.e. you) is suitable for the job, is made in the first three minutes of the interview! That is why your physical appearance is so important.

● Be on time

Next, make sure that you get there in good time. If you get held up en route you must try to get to a phone box and explain that you're going to be late, rather than simply turning up long after the interview was scheduled to start. It's always better to arrive early rather than late. Aim to be there at least a quarter of an hour ahead of time, even though the odds are that the interviews will be running a bit late. Getting there early means you'll have time to relax (by taking deep breaths) and get used to the surroundings. It also means that if the building is hard to find you've allowed a bit of time for getting lost!

- **Try to relax**

Remember that everyone is nervous before an interview. It's not just you! An experienced interviewer will expect you to be uneasy at first. They'll make allowances for it and will make every effort to help you get into a state where you can show what you're capable of. A few minutes into the interview, and you should be starting to relax. Who knows, you may even begin to enjoy the opportunity of talking about yourself for half an hour!

- **Be yourself**

Remember also that interviews are not intended to be interrogations of poor helpless victims by cruel and heartless Personnel Managers! It is their job to get the best out of you, as it is yours to see that they succeed from the moment you walk into the room.

What will happen

1) When the interviewer introduces him or herself to you, shake hands, smile and respond to whatever introductory comment is made to you. If the interviewer says "Pleased to meet you", or "Welcome to X, my name is . . . ", you can reply "Pleased to meet you". Remember to speak clearly and establish eye contact. Whatever you do, keep your head up and avoid mumbling.

2) The interview may well start with the interviewer trying to put you at ease by asking you questions such as, "Did you find us easily?" or even, "Isn't it a lovely day?". It may not be scintillating conversation, but they're trying to help you, so humour them! Show that you can play the small-talk game as well as the next

person. The stage is now set for the start of the real interview.

3) The first few questions are likely to be related to what you wrote on your application form or CV. The interviewer will want you to expand on some things, and to clarify others. Next, in a typical interview, will come questions designed to discover what sort of person you are. The interviewer will be interested in finding out what makes you tick, what motivates you, etc. With your skills of self-analysis tuned to perfect pitch with the help of this book, you should have no trouble answering convincingly!

We presented a list of questions that you may be asked during an interview. If you had an answer for each of them, then it's unlikely that you'll be caught out by any question. However, some interviewers may be more imaginative. You should be grateful. It shows they're taking the interview – and you – seriously. Try and respond to new questions with answers that show that you're prepared to be original too.

For some jobs you may be asked technical questions, so it's worth looking over a few basic things before you go in. If this is the case, it's likely that they will give you advance warning. If it's the kind of interview where you would expect technical questions but they haven't mentioned it in their letter, why not phone to ask about the format of the interview. It can't do any harm, and it may allow you to prepare.

INTERVIEW TIPS

Here are a few tips to your help you make the most of your interview:

1) Try to avoid simple "Yes" or "No" answers. Give examples, expand on the question – anything to avoid an uneasy 'staccato' sort of conversation.

2) Don't feel that you have to reply to a question immediately. If you need to think about it for a while, let the interviewer know, and take your time about answering. It's an unusual but extremely effective tactic which suggests that you are not just thoughtful, but determined.

3) If you're not sure about what the interviewer is getting at, politely tell them so. At the end of a long day, the interviewer may not be expressing him or herself entirely clearly. It's perfectly in order for you to say: "I'm sorry, I'm not sure I understand you. Do you mean . . . ?" The interviewer will then repeat the question in a different way. With luck, this time you'll understand it and they will again be impressed by your courage and determination not to talk nonsense.

4) Concentrate on the quality rather than the quantity of your answers and comments. In other words, don't waffle. Give them what they need to know and a little bit extra besides. If the person interviewing shows signs of restlessness, looking away, looking at papers, shuffling papers, etc., it probably means that you're talking too much. Bear in mind that in a well conducted interview, the interviewer-candidate speaking ratio should be roughly 30/70.

You may be asked about how you would behave in a hypothetical situation. Here's an example. "Suppose you were in a shop and an irate customer started demanding a refund for a faulty product when you've been told by management only to exchange goods, not give refunds. What would you do?" The trick is to think back to an occasion when this, or something like this, has happened to you. How did you react – did you panic or keep your cool? Relate this to the original question, if what you did on the real occasion was the best way to deal with it. If it wasn't, re-tell the story but this time slightly amend it to present yourself in a more favourable light.

Research shows that both interviewer and candidate feel that the interview has gone best if they have established a link between them, i.e. they've discovered they have something in common. The interviewer is more likely to be the person to discover the link, since they will have access to your life history. But see if you can help them, by picking up on any clues they offer about their interests and concerns, especially when they coincide with yours.

Inevitably you will have some bad interviews, where you feel that you haven't put yourself across well, and that the chemistry between you and the interviewer just wasn't right. Don't blame yourself. Put it down to experience. The only exception is when you feel certain that you have been unfairly discriminated against. In this case, you could contact the Equal Opportunities Commission. Your local Citizens Advice Bureau will be able to help you here.

If a company asks you to attend two interviews, the first one will probably be fairly short. Its function will be to allow them to check you out and vice versa. It is unusual for candidates to be subjected to a really testing interview at this stage in the game. But even if the depth of the interview surprises you, you should be adequately prepared for it by now.

TO ACCEPT . . . OR NOT

The final stage in the whole job-hunting process is to find out what to do if you're offered the job. Obvious enough you might think, but have you really thought it through? If you're sure that the job's for you, then go right ahead and accept it. If you're fairly sure but have a few niggling doubts, phone the company and chat to someone who could help sort out these worries for you. There are drawbacks to just about every job, but you will need to be convinced that the balance between the disadvantages and advantages is tipped firmly in favour of the latter before accepting.

If you feel at the end of this book that you still have no idea what you want out of life, what kind of job you'd like and so on, it may be an idea to get some professional vocational guidance. This can be a fairly expensive process. Currently it would cost you around £200. A lot of people have commented that really all this kind of counselling does is to confirm what you already know. If, however, you decide that you are totally lost and really need professional help in deciding what careers you should be looking at, make sure that the company you approach is professional. Ideally you should use an organisation someone you know has successfully consulted.

Here we are then at the end of the whole process. We hope you've enjoyed racking your brains over the quizzes and tests. But more than that, we hope you've actually gained a real insight into yourself – what sort of person you really are, your likes/dislikes, and your hopes and dreams. We feel sure that you'll be able to find at least one job you're well suited to, according to your own personal skills, interests and personality.

It's all down to you now! Make a start today by researching the jobs you've pinpointed. What qualifications do you need? Which are the best companies to work for? Is your C.V. up to date? Did you know that, because of the fall in numbers of 16 to 19 year olds, there are going to be many more opportunities for employment, training, and education for YOU? So think positive, go out there and grab the job you want.

One thing to remember when choosing your career is the old saying:

'If you don't know where you're going, you'll end up somewhere else!'

If you're not careful, that 'somewhere else' could be the dole queue or a job you really hate. But you **are** careful! You've taken the trouble to read this book, which suggests that you're going to choose your career logically and with careful consideration. Now go ahead and prove us right.

SUMMARY

In this chapter we looked at the interview process.

WE COVERED:

Preparation for the interview:
- how to research the company.
- questions you may be asked on the day.
- what the interviewer is looking for.
- tests you may have to take, and how to deal with them.
- questions you would like to ask.

The interview itself:
- how to conduct yourself.
- tips on making the most of your interview.
- what to do after a bad interview.
- what to do when you're not sure if you want the job offered to you.

CHAPTER 7:
MAKING YOUR JOB WORK FOR YOU

Let's suppose that you've read this book and discovered enough about yourself to land the job of your dreams. What should your next step be?

Moving from school or college into the world of work will have a huge effect on your life. Suddenly, you really do have to get yourself out of bed in the morning and in to work. You have to learn to dress properly, and to manage your money. Maybe you'll even have to cope with living away from home for the first time. It all spells **independence** – the real difference between childhood and adulthood.

READY, STEADY, GO

Independence can be a daunting prospect. No amount of careful planning can prepare you for what it actually feels like to be in a new environment, surrounded by strangers, not knowing where you're supposed to be when, or what is expected of you. But there is a lot you can do to soften the initial blow and to accelerate the moment when the uncertainty of your new life suddenly starts to look like an avenue lined with opportunities instead of a threatening voyage into the unknown.

For example, it's a good idea to take a break before any major change in life, though it isn't sensible to be away right up to the last moment before you start your new job. If you can't quite stretch to a week in Acapulco, a few days staying with friends in the country or just lounging around at home will do the trick just as well. The idea is to give yourself a chance to get used to some of the changes in your life, before diving into the deep end.

If you're going to leave home for the first time, then you'll need a few weeks to get organised. Think carefully about whether or not you want to leave home so soon. Moving into a dingy basement room may not prove to be the haven of peace that you expected. You might be better off staying at home for a few months until you sort out your finances and can do your house hunting properly.

If your work is too far away for you to stay at home, or if you really feel it's time to make the break, the important thing is to do your research. First of all, decide what area you want to live in, taking into consideration things like public transport, proximity to shops and entertainment, and the price of accommodation. Then buy the local papers, look in local shop windows and talk to estate agents about the kinds of accommodation available. Visit a few before making your decision and take a friend along with you, just in case you're seeing them through rose coloured spectacles.

Most importantly, don't bite off more than you can chew financially. Work out how much you can easily afford, and stick to it. Remember you'll probably have to pay rates, electricity, phone bills, etc as well. As a rule of thumb, you should expect to spend between a quarter and a third of your income on a place to live.

MONEY TALKS

One of the biggest changes you'll experience at this stage in your life, is in the amount of money you have at your disposal. Unless you worked every evening and every weekend of your school days, you should suddenly have much more money to spend. How you manage this money could have a major impact on your happiness.

You have probably heard the old saying 'Money talks'. But have you ever wondered what it says about you? How much money you have, how easy you find it to keep a grip on your personal finances, whether you use money or it uses you – these are issues which affect every aspect of your dealings with the world. And it doesn't matter whether we're talking about a City slicker deciding when to replace the Porsche or someone working in a High Street store, trying to save for a snazzy new hair cut. The sums involved are much less important than a person's attitude towards money, because this can make the difference between happiness and despair in your new job.

To discover what your approach to money is, read through the following pairs of statements, and tick whichever one of each pair seems to you to be more true. In some cases, you may find yourself agreeing or disagreeing to varying degrees with both statements. When this happens, tick whichever of the statements is closer to your opinion.

Tick one of each pair of boxes

1. (a) Most people could learn to make money if they really tried. ☐
or (b) Some people get rich and some don't – it's a matter of luck. ☐

2. (a) I may never become a millionaire but I reckon I'll always be able to make the money I really need. ☐
or (b) Who knows if I'll ever become rich? It's all down to chance, like winning the football pools. ☐

3. (a) There's no mystery about money – it's mostly acquired by brains or hard work. ☐
or (b) Money moves in mysterious ways – you can never predict when you'll have it and when you won't. ☐

4. (a) Whenever I need money for something I can usually lay my hands on it somehow. ☐
or (b) When I need money for something, sometimes the money appears and sometimes it doesn't. ☐

5. (a) I like using my head to work out ways of making more money. ☐

or (b) In an arcade where there are cash prizes, ☐
I'd rather play a game of chance than a
game of skill.

To interpret your response to these questions, you need to understand that the human race can be divided into two categories: **Controllers** – people who feel that they have a real say in their own destiny – and fatalists – those who reckon that what happens to them is mostly due to factors beyond their control. This important aspect of personality can be seen very clearly in people's attitude towards money.

If you gave mostly – i.e. 3 or more – (a) answers to the questions above, you are a Controller. Where financial matters are concerned, Controllers are at an advantage. They believe they can make money work for them, rather than simply being forced to react to financial pressures. Controllers know that money is simply a tool, invented by the human race for its own convenience. They accept that money needs to be used and made to work for them rather than be allowed to dominate or oppress them. If you're a Controller you're unlikely to find it difficult to cope with the financial issues working life throws up. In fact you'll probably thrive under the challenge.

If on the other hand most – i.e. 3 or more – of your answers to Questions 15 were (b)s, at the moment you are a Fatalist. Fatalists are at a disadvantage in financial affairs because when they have money they don't claim the credit they deserve for earning it, and when they don't, they complain of life's unfairness instead of working out what needs to be done to remedy the situation. Of course there can be an element of luck about acquiring money. Some people do win the Pools, just as others inherit vast fortunes. But it's a better policy to concentrate on the fact that other people who start off with no more money than you have are able to exert more control over the state of their finances. Some people always seem to have the cash when they really need it. Is there any reason why you shouldn't be one of them?

ACTION STATIONS

Preparing to deal with your money is not the only thing you can do to make the transition from school or college a little easier. It's also a good idea to put some work into preparing for the job itself. You've obviously impressed your employers with your charm and charisma at the interview, so how do you live up to their high expectations?

A few days before you start, check the times of the local buses or trains, and plan your journey to work. Be generous in your estimates, and leave time for emergencies like broken down buses, and getting lost. Arriving late on your first day doesn't give a very good impression, and you won't be on top form if you've had to sprint from the bus stop!

Another important consideration when you're getting ready for the first day, is 'what will I wear?'. Again, do some research. Find out how you will be expected to dress, and plan accordingly. In some organisations, you will be regarded with horror and suspicion if you're not wearing a suit and tie, or a smart dress, while in others it's quite acceptable to do your own thing and wear your Afghan coat and Jesus sandles! Make sure you get it right.

YOUR STRESS RATING

However no matter how thoroughly you prepare for a new job, there's always a certain amount of stress involved. This is because all changes are stressful. But some of us make things worse by the way we approach life. To find out how much unnecessary pressure you impose on yourself, try the following quiz.

In each of the following questions you must decide which of the alternatives, a or b, is more true for you. There is no in between category. Just tick whichever statement seems to apply more accurately.

1. Are you a) casual about appointments ☐
   or b) never late? ☐

2. Are you a) very competitive ☐
   or b) not competitive? ☐

3. Are you a) a good listener ☐
   or b) do you interrupt often? ☐

4. Are you a) always rushed ☐
   or b) never rushed? ☐

5. Can you a) wait patiently ☐
   or b) are you impatient? ☐

6. Do you a) tend to hide your feelings ☐
   or b) usually express what you feel? ☐

7. Do you a) take things one at a time □
   or b) do lots of things at once? □

8. Would you describe yourself as a) hard driving □
   or b) easy going? □

9. Do you tend to a) do things slowly □
   (eg eating or walking)
   or b) do things fast? □

10. Do you a) have few interests outside work □
    or b) have lots of interests outside work? □

Now let's see how you score. For the odd numbered questions (1, 3 etc) score 2 points for every tick you have in a b) box. For the even-numbered questions, score 2 points for every a) answer. The higher your score, the more stress you are imposing on yourself. If you have a score of 16 or more, you really need to take active steps to reduce the burden you are imposing on yourself. A score in the 12-16 range indicates a fair degree of ambitiousness and concern with time. A score of 5-11 suggests that you are fairly relaxed in your approach to life. A score of 4 or less means that you are not merely 'laid-back' but almost horizontal!

JOB SATISFACTION

If you scored less than 6 you can skip this section of the chapter and move on to look at making the most of your job. If your score was more than 6, read on. Are there any obvious reasons for you being so stressed at the moment? Do you suspect that it's your job that's getting you down, and that it would all be alright again if you could only go back to school? Be careful, it's all too easy to blame unhappiness on your job when actually your main problems lie outside the office doors. As it's so important that you identify the cause of your stress correctly before you put any plans together for dealing with it, try this quiz to find out just how big a part your job plays.

Once again you should answer either TRUE or FALSE for each statement, depending on whether or not it's an accurate impression of your feelings and attitudes.

TRUE/FALSE

1. If I won the Pools, I certainly wouldn't ☐ ☐
   carry on working where I am now.

2. The most important things that happen ☐ ☐
   to me involve work.

3. I try to think of ways of doing my job ☐ ☐
   more effectively.

4. When I get into difficulty at work, ☐ ☐
   there's no one I can turn to for help.

5. Even if another employer offered me a ☐ ☐
   lot of money, I would not seriously
   think of changing my present job.

6. In all honesty, I couldn't advise a ☐ ☐
   friend to join my company.

7. I often find myself looking on a day's ☐ ☐
   work with a sense of a job well done.

8. I am too embarrassed to tell people who I work for. ☐ ☐

9. If I had my life over again, I wouldn't choose to do the job I'm doing. ☐ ☐

10. It makes me unhappy when my work is not up to its usual standard. ☐ ☐

Now let's find out if you're happy in your work. For questions 2, 3, 5, 7 and 10, score 2 points for each TRUE answer, and zero for each FALSE. For questions 1, 4, 6, 8 and 9, score 2 points for each FALSE and zero for each TRUE. The higher your score, the more satisfied you are. A score of 12 or more suggests that you find your job rewarding in a psychological as well as a financial sense; a score of 6 or less indicates that you are getting less pleasure from it than most people – and less than is healthy for you.

MORALE BOOSTERS

If your job is getting you down, what can you do about it? First of all, you should examine your outlook on life. A negative outlook on life will colour all your successes, and enlarge your failures out of all proportion. If your confidence is at an all-time low, try looking back at the list you made in Chapter 3 of all your skills. See, you do have worthwhile and useful skills of all sorts!

Once you've mastered the art of looking on the bright side, the next step in beating work stress is to take some positive action. You need to identify exactly what bits of your job are making you stressed.

Keep a diary for a week or so. Note down all the different activities you get involved in each day, and record how stressed they made you feel on a scale of 0-5. If they are easily accomplished and give you no problems give them a score of 0. On the other hand, if they make you want to rush off to the loo screaming, give them a score of 5.

When you have carried out this exercise for a whole week, look at all the tasks you scored as '5' on the stress scale. Ask yourself how you can reduce the amount of stress these tasks cause you. For example, maybe you don't have enough knowledge to carry out the task effectively. If that's the case, ask someone in the know to help you out.

Set yourself goals and priorities for dealing with each '5' stress factor, and dates by which you hope to achieve some improvement. When you've made some headway with these stress factors, move on to those on your list which scored 4, and so on.

If, after carrying out this exercise, you still feel that you haven't quite cracked the stress problem, try to remember the following four general rules for beating stress:

1. Only do one thing at a time.

2. Don't expect perfection – from yourself or from other people. It's an impossible dream which will only make you feel frustrated and resentful.

3. Make yourself take breaks, even when you're working to a deadline.

4. Fight stress by taking exercise, relaxing, laughing and doing anything you actively enjoy.

PERSONALITY CLASHES

Of course, it's not just the job itself that can cause stress. The worst offender is a human being, the one whose office at the end of the corridor bears the legend – MANAGER.

The difficult boss is a very common species! No matter how much you try you just can't seem to keep them happy. Try and work out whether it's only you who has this problem with the boss. If the rest of your colleagues seem to be getting on well with him or her, think about what it is you could be doing wrong. The next time your boss snaps at you, think about what preceded it. Do you have a way of interacting with them which gets up their nose? Do you, for example, pretend everything is going well when the company is about to collapse around you? If you can't see any pattern in the way you and your boss deal with each other, ask them what they feel is wrong with your work. Listen to what they say, and try and put any reasonable requests for change in to action.

If, on the other hand, your boss behaves badly with everyone in the company, ask yourself if they are under a lot of pressure from their superiors at the moment. Or perhaps they have problems in their private life which they are bringing into work with them. Try and get to know your boss a little better, listen sensitively when he/she gets bad tempered, and see if you can find ways of helping them out. Of course it could just be that your boss is an unreasonably bad tempered person. If so you may have to enlist the support of colleagues in trying to get them to change their ways.

Colleagues can also make life pretty unpleasant for the 'new girl' or 'new boy'. The company old hands may have formed themselves into little cliques, which seem impossible to penetrate. The best way to deal with this kind of situation is to be open and friendly. Ask your colleagues about themselves and try to find common interests. Be patient, and as they get to know you better they will become less suspicious.

Be aware of your own personality – especially those aspects of it that have got you into trouble in the past (a quick temper perhaps, or being too eager to please, too willing to pass the buck, or whatever). Then use your skills as a personality analyst on your new colleagues. Form hypotheses about what they are like, but make sure you test them thoroughly before accepting them. First impressions can be deceptive, and you don't want to find yourself trying to win someone over with an approach designed for a quite different sort of animal! Remember the old motto, 'different strokes for different folks'.

Finally, remember that everyone feels at least a little stressed and anxious in their first few months in a new job. When it's also your **first** job, the challenge is even greater. Give yourself a chance to adapt to all the changes that working life brings by sticking it out for at least six months. Put our hints about managing your finances, and dealing with stress into practice. Allow time not just to come to terms with the mechanics of your job and the tasks it involves, but also with the people alongside whom you have to work.

Suppose though that, despite all your efforts, you just can't crack the difficult boss, or that your colleagues are making your life miserable, what should your next step be? Whatever it is, don't act too hastily. However bad things seem, you must serve out your notice.

SECOND TIME AROUND

Once you've made up your mind to go, you'll find your attention switching away from the irritations of today's job towards the challenges of tomorrow's. So before you forget the details, why not try to make the most of your final weeks by analysing what went wrong. That way, you have a better chance of making sure that you don't make the same mistakes twice. Why did you take the job in the first place, and in what ways has it failed to live up to your expectations? The chances are you'll find you misjudged either the job or some aspect of yourself. The whole point of this book has been to help improve your judgement of both. So why not take a second look at those relevant chapters.

A cynic once described second marriage as a triumph of hope over experience! If you use the experience of your first crack at the world of work constructively, you should be in a position to rely on something more substantial than hope next time round.

SUGGESTED READING

Here are a few other books in which you might find useful hints and suggestions for stress-free job hunting!

General Guides to Job Hunting

A Guide to Post-school Opportunities by Felicity Taylor (Kogan Page, 1981).

Working It Out, Careers and Occupational Information Centre (available from COIC Sales Dept, Freepost, Sheffield SL1 4BR).

Job Finding: A Step by Step Guide by Penny Hacket (John Murray, 1983).

The Job-finders' Book by Ruth Sandys and Alexa Stace (Kogan Page, 1979).

Get That Job, Manpower Services Commissions (leaflet available from Job Centres or MSC, Sheffield S1 4PQ).

Getting the Right Job by Chris Parsons and Angela Neustatter (Pan Books, 1979).

Getting to Know Yourself

Know Your Own Personality by H. J. Eysenck and Glenn Wilson (Penguin, 1976).

Check Your Own IQ by H. J. Eysenck (Penguin, 1983).

Interviews

Facing the Interview: a guide to self-preparation and presentation by Clive Fletcher (Unwin, 1981).

How to be Interviewed by D. Mackenzie Davey and P. McDonnel (British Institute of Management, 1980).

Talk Yourself Into a Job by Chris Webb (Macmillan 1979).

How to Succeed at an Interview, and How to Survive if You Don't by Kris Box and Don Cole (EP Publishing Ltd, 1982).

Coping With Interviews by Martin Higham (New Opportunities Press, 1983).

Coping with Working Life

All This and Work Too – The Psychology of Office Life by Dr Maryon Tysoe (Fontana/Collins, 1988).